NO TIME
FOR DYING

Voices of Retirement

Edited
by
Joan Thornton

Yorkshire Art Circus
1989

Published by Yorkshire Art Circus,
13-15 Sagar Street, Castleford,
West Yorkshire WF10 1AG
Telephone 0977 550401

© Yorkshire Art Circus 1989
© Cover design: Wayne Clarida and Linda McGillivray
© Commissioned photographs: Stephen McClarence
Tyepsetting: Wordstream Ltd.
Printing: FM Repro Ltd., Ravensthorpe, Dewsbury, W. Yorkshire

Editorial team:

Margaret Allott	Adrian Gray	Brian Lewis
John Chapman	Evelyn Haythorne	Harry Malkin
Ian Clayton	Carol Hill	Linda McGillivray
Olive Fowler	Janet Hilton	Iris Taylor

ISBN 0 947780 49 1

Yorkshire Art Circus is a unique book publisher. We link our books with performances and exhibitions and offer workshops for the first time writer.
Yorkshire Art Circus projects have successfully toured Community Centres, colleges, galleries, clubs, galas and Art Centres. In all our work we bring new artists to new audiences.

For details of our programme of performances, exhibitions, conferences and workshops send for our brochure and book list at the address above.

DONCASTER LIBRARY SERVICE

CONTENTS

Working on the wall hanging

INTRODUCTION

This book is one of four projects sponsored jointly by the Yorkshire Art Circus and Doncaster Library Services, which began in Balby, South Yorkshire in January 1989. A wall hanging, and collections of work by an artist and a photographer, all sharing the common theme of 'life after retirement' have been produced in conjunction with the book, to be exhibited at its launch and afterwards tour South Yorkshire.

The Marshalls Residential Home for the elderly was the starting point for collécting photographs and stories then the net spread much wider to catch a full range of attitudes and experiences of retirement. Gold prospectors, windsurfers and pilots tended to be more difficult to track down and were inclined to be too busy doing, to spend much time talking. However there are ways and means and while one interview was conducted swimming alongside the contributor another took place at two thousand feet in a Cessna.

Some of the photographs by Stephen McClarence, prepared for the photographic exhibition and some taken by the artist Harry Malkin, as inspiration for his pictures are also included. The spectacular appliqued wall hanging, ten by six feet in size, produced by Linda McGillivray, assisted by residents of The Marshalls - a work of art itself — is reproduced on the cover of this book.

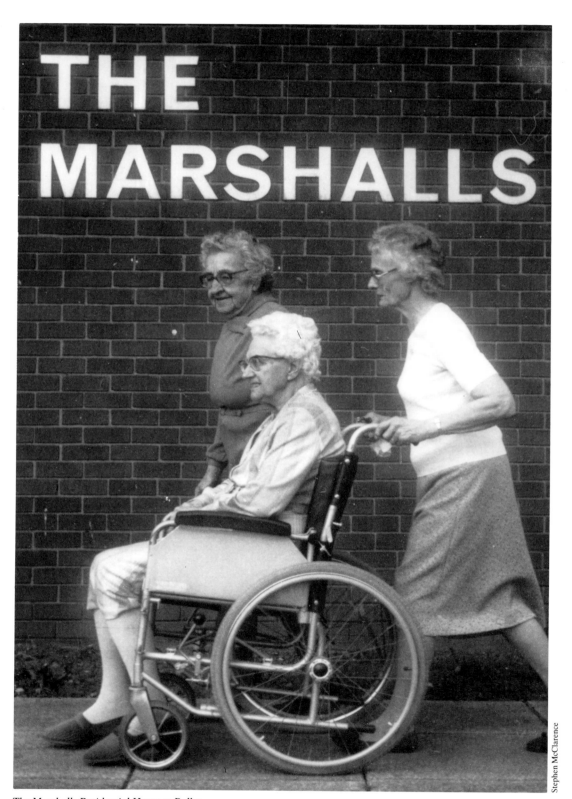

The Marshalls Residential Home at Balby

Many thanks to the following people who have contributed their stories to this book:

Ivy Able
Ellen Axup
Connie Baistow
Winifred Baker
Wilfred Barker
Ruby Bartle
Elsie Barton
Gladys Bellamy
Gerty Birbett
Cyril Bland
Muriel Blanshard
Winifred Bolton
Arthur Bone
Vera Burdoch
Agnes Burton
Ann Caperness
Nora Carter
Paddy Cavanagh
Amelia Cawthorne
Fred Clarke
Peggie Clarke
Alice Cofield
Monica College
Vera Cooper
Jessie Coster
Bella Crooks
Kathy Evans

Mary Fanshaw
Joan Fletcher
Ruth Franklin
John Garraughty
Bernard Gilbert
Nora Gilbert
Horace Green
Nellie Hancock
Eric Haythorne
Evelyn Haythorne
Emily Heal
Susie Hoggett
Gordon Howard
Jack Hulme
Evelyn Lavin
Edith Lear
Elma Leask
Bill Lewins
Bessie Lightfoot
Jacob Lowther
Christie Macleod
Sam Martin
Steve McGlynn
Doris Mashford
Clifford Micklethwaite
Gertie Micklethwaite
Ernest Mills

Adrian Morris
Eve Nixon
Elizabeth O'Brien
Jim O'Brien
Edna Pinder
Kathleen Pogmore
Reg Pogmore
William Ponberth
Glen Pybus
Elizabeth Robinson
Elsie Sayles
Kathleen Shillitoe
Bessie Smith
Elsie Smith
Marie Smith
Olive Smith
Edna Stone
Hannah Taylor
Kate Thirkill
Alice Tomlinson
Lilly Walker
Alan Wheeliker
Ivy Williamson
Doris Wood
Ned Wright
Harry Yorke
Ray Yoxall

Our thanks also to the many other individuals and organisations who helped make this book possible:

Joan Sisman and the staff at Balby Library
The staff of Doncaster Library Services
The staff of The Marshalls Residential Home
Doncaster Local History Library for The Bagshaw Collection.
Yorkshire Arts

*I'm not half enjoying
my retirement*

Six Decades Shalt Thou Labour And Rest On The Seventh

The Best Of Times

☐ I've another year to retirement and I can't wait. I'm really looking forward to it. So many people seem to dread it, as if their life is virtually over once they've finished work, but I've a lot of interests and never enough time. When I'm retired I intend to have a go at lots of new interests as well as taking up some of my old hobbies again.

I want to build another plane. I've already built a small bi- plane — it took me about six years but I got it in the air last year. It's great to fly it but the real pleasure was in the building of it. The next plane will be a two seater instead of one seater; that way my wife will be able to come with me and we'll be able to go off on jaunts around the country, from one airfield to another.

It's my ambition to fly myself to Spain. We have a small villa out there, near Fuengirola on the Costa del Sol. We had it built with retirement in mind, though I don't think we'll retire to live there permanently like a lot of British people do. Our family and roots are here in England and anyway the summers are too hot over there. It would be nice to be able to go for five or six months every winter and rent it out in the summer. To fly to Spain in my present plane would take a few days with a dozen stop-overs to refuel because it's about 1800 miles, and though the plane does about thirty miles to the gallon, it's only a five gallon tank. So perhaps I'll not attempt that feat till I've built a larger plane.

Once in Spain I also plan to build a boat instead of lazing around sun-bathing. Then I'd take up sea fishing as a new hobby and catch our own food — well some of it — maybe. I shall take up geology again, I studied it in my youth and maintained a passing interest in it but there's a lot more I would like to learn — and the same goes for botany. That's a subject that has always

interested me and I've promised myself that I'll take it up as a serious hobby when I retire. And Spanish, of course I'll have to learn Spanish. Me and my wife started learning at night school about five years ago, when we first got the idea of a villa in Spain. Peggie is getting on all right with Spanish but I'm going to have to put more work in to it. I've no head for languages.

I also intend to do more walking and more golf. I'll probably be able to combine the two. I'll have to spend more time looking for lost golf balls because I won't be able to afford to buy so many. And perhaps we shall get a touring caravan and travel all round England and Europe when we make our regular six monthly trek to and from southern Spain. And perhaps some of these are pipedreams but I hope we never get too old to dream.

Our greatest concern is that our health holds out because we've no time for dying, not for a long time yet — there's too many things we want to do first.

☐ I'm sixty-one and still working but the milestone marked Senior Citizen is on the horizon and I hope soon to exchange paid work for voluntary work. Do you remember being asked, when you were young, "What do you want to do when you grow up?" The choice seemed infinite and the sky was the limit.

I ask myself a similar question now. Do I offer my services to Adult Literacy? I've always enjoyed reading so I'd like to help someone else to the same pleasure. I've always enjoyed using my hands so I would enjoy helping handicapped people to develop skills in any sort of light crafts. Shall I offer my services to Marriage Guidance and go for training? In my working career I've seen so many disturbed children from broken homes that I feel it would be a worthwhile service. Should I go and work at one of the charity shops in town? I like a gossip and I think I'd enjoy that.

For the last twenty years I've also promised myself a camera with a zoom lens to photograph butterflies and birds. So I could join a camera club. Maybe I'll join first without a camera and see if it suits me. Faces have always fascinated me and I'd like to learn to paint portraits in oil. When I'd acquired enough skill I'd paint my own family portraits. I have some sepia photographs of my ancestors so I could paint my very own rogues' gallery.

I could go on and on because there's lots of things I haven't done yet and as I've always been a late developer, I'm optimistic enough to think there's still plenty of time to make up my mind — or try them all.

☐   I've never had so much fun since I retired. I've been abroad three times with the old folk from the centre. We look for the cheapest holidays and take as many as we can. I can't afford for my husband to go as well, but he's a happy soul in his garden, he's like an old sheep.

☐   For me, the perfect retirement will be to live like this lady I knew — she was a real character. She always wore a huge poncho with trousers and bright coloured tops. Her hair was bleached and she wore it in a tight top knot. Her glasses had tilting sun-glasses fixed on to them which she wore winter and summer alike.

She had a great variety of hobbies. At first it was pottery, she got so involved in it at art college, she decided to do her potting at home as well. The car was turned out of the garage and she invested in a kiln and a potter's wheel. The pots she turned out were original and great designs.

After that phase wore off she went into fabric design and die painting, and then the art college found a huge weaving loom in the cellars of the college, they set this up for her in a room on the top floor of the college. She read up on the art of weaving and spent hours perfecting the technique; it was a slow process at first. It was quite a wonderful experience to watch her design the fabric on paper and then set about weaving it. She didn't make yards of the material, just enough for a skirt or a poncho, which she made up herself. She could really put her hand to anything.

I visited her a few times in her home, that was quite an event. She always put the kettle on straight away but the tea was never P G Tips or Typhoo it was jasmine tea or camomile or some sort of exotic brew. With this she served saffron biscuits — home made of course. On one occasion she asked me to go for a cup of tea I took a friend with me, she was much younger than me and didn't have much tact. When tea duly came she had a sip and spluttered it out shouting, "God what is it — pee?"

☐   To me, growing old is about getting as much out of life while we are able. My life is a lot different from my mum's — she knew nothing but hard work and poverty. When I look at my automatic machine and Hoover I often think of her bent over the old wash tub with a scrubbing brush. She took washing in for a living — had to, we kids needed keeping. Yes, hard work killed her. I don't intend it doing the same to me though.

☐   At seventy-three, my friend is so full of energy and enthusiasm for life and that's just how I want to be in my old age — active and always ready to try new things. Perhaps retirement is just a reflection of your earlier life. If you are physically and mentally active and always ready to try new things, old age is a long time coming. But some folk are middle- aged by their thirties and old in their forties and that's appalling when these days you're likely to live till you're eighty or more.

My friend took up windsurfing when he was seventy and he's still doing it on the local reservoir where they do sailing and canoeing. He is also a keen walker and cyclist. He goes on cycling holidays to France for a couple of weeks every year with his daughter.

He's been all things in his time — an actor

Traditional retirement for some

Stephen McClarence

at the Old Vic, a policeman, a mind reader's stooge touring theatres all over the country. He was the one who mingled with the audience and obtained personal possessions and then gave the mind reader a clue — "take your time" meant it was a watch that he was holding. The last job he had started as a labourer but he was Company Secretary by the time he retired.

His wife was the catcher in a trapeze act with her sister, who was the flyer. Unfortunately his wife is crippled with arthritis now and can't join him in his active retirement and all the hobbies he's taken up. The circus that his wife worked for offered them a tiger cub when the circus was planning to go abroad. They kept it in a run at the back garden but it had the run of the house. They kept it till it died of old age.

He drives a Volvo and regularly goes off to the Dales or Lakes for a few days with sleeping bag and primus stove. He sleeps in the back of the car. I've got tremendous admiration for him — except he's a terrible driver. He and his wife were out for a drive, they were in the middle of nowhere, not a soul in sight and he reversed into the only other car for miles around. Neither is he averse to doing a 180 degree turn at full speed if he changes his mind while he's driving along.

☐ I grow old day by day, good or bad, but I don't saddle myself with a load of worries. Had enough of that when I was young. My advice to anyone is:

> See all, hear all, say nowt,
> Eat all, sup all, pay nowt.
> If a person should drunken roam,
> It's your duty to see him home
> And say nowt.

The Worst Of Times

☐ Growing old is a fact of life and it's no good trying to hide it under a pillow. We just have to accept it, but I couldn't do what a lot of the old ones do; sit in the Arndale Centre all day. It's a shame when old people have to go out of their homes armed with a flask and sandwiches to get a bit of warmth and light. The poor sods have no other way to save on their bills.

☐ I remember the Cadeby pit explosion in 1912. My friend's husband was killed in it. I also remember the sinking of the Lusitania in 1916 and the Liberal government being in power. There hasn't been a Liberal government since. I also remember very well the 1926 strike. Churchill was a minister then and he said he would make the strikers eat grass. And we very nearly did, but I managed to go radish picking, I used to get tuppence for two hundred bunches.

I've had a hard life, but I haven't shoved it behind a door, I've got on with it. I think Churchill and Thatcher are the two worst leaders England has ever known. And who was Hitler? An evil little upstart painter.

☐ Though I like it here in The Marshalls, I wish I could do more. A day can be a long time when you can't do anything. The only thing I can do now is grow old gracefully.

☐ It's nice to grow old gracefully, but a lot of us don't. I live day to day and I'm happy when I get up in a morning. I try to help folk but I get really fed up with some of them in this home, when they won't help themselves in the dining room and what have you.

☐ I hate being retired. My old man is quite content to potter about and make his model galleons. I can't sit still. If it wasn't for my bad back I'd be doing a lot more than I am.

☐ My mother-in-law always runs her home like a hotel. They have the front room that's done out every week from top to bottom, but her husband isn't allowed in it at all. When he retired, he never felt comfortable, he felt as if he was in the way all the time. His wife made no bones about telling him so either.

☐ I like to go to Hallgate Reform Church on a Sunday morning but when I go, there's only two of us on the Traction bus and I'm frightened the bus company might take it off. Then I won't be able to go.

☐ Old people get looked on as a liability these days. Lloyd George said he'd make this land fit for heroes and look at us now. We did all the fighting and we're the poorest pensioners in Europe. You've got a situation with some old folk where they have to decide whether to have a fire or a cooked meal. That can't be right, surely?

☐ I'd love to get up on a morning and know I had something to do. I thought about putting an advert in the paper for baby-sitting or taking ironing in, but if I put 'pensioner' they'd imagine somebody with a stick.

☐ I didn't think the time would come when I would sit gazing into space, but I do. Sometimes I sit doing nothing for ages. I look at the street lamp outside, when it comes on I switch mine on, then I switch on the television. Before television we had only heard about far off places in books and on maps. Now we've got all the troubles of the world in our front room everyday.

☐ I used to like going to Gilbert and Sullivan but I can't go now unless there's a matinee. My neighbour started me off over forty years ago. My husband said at the time, "What do you want to see that rubbish for?" But I went and loved it. I'd still like to go now but I'm petrified to go out at night.

It's a terrible world when you can't walk down your own street in the dark. I'm frightened to death of youngsters. It's not long since I went to buy a clock at Argos; the Arndale centre was full of boys and girls with their hair sticking up. Scared me to death.

Mind you I think television and the

Traditional retirement for others

13

newspapers help to terrify us, always full of murder, muggings and vandals. It's a terrible world we live in.

☐ Kids are a lot more outgoing than we were. We were much more timid. Most of us had inferiority complexes and a terrible lack of confidence. Now the youngsters are full of themselves, full of confidence, no qualms about talking to anybody. That's the main difference between the young of our day and now. But with it seems to have come a lack of respect, foul language and aggressive behaviour. Call me old fashioned, but surely that's wrong.

☐ The young of today think they've got a monopoly on wild behaviour. Some of us were pretty strong characters ourselves, you know. You don't chain yourselves to railings and throw yourselves under horses if you are a wimp.

☐ I fear that the National Health is going for a burton and the thought of having to pay for treatment if I'm sick, well, it really frightens me.

☐ When you get older, reminiscing is all a lot of people have left. It seems to keep them happy but we're not all content with that. I like company and I get lonely like a lot of older people do. Apart from lack of money, loneliness is the worst enemy of old age. It's the cause of depression in a lot of older folk. It's almost like an illness itself; looking at the clock and it never moves, locking the door, opening it, getting the insurance money ready hours before he comes, going to bed out of the way.

☐ I can tell you what's up with the world today, there's not enough laughter. A lot of people are too busy reporting each other up at the DHSS. They don't like to see anybody getting anything they're not getting. And all this mugging and hooliganism, it makes my stomach sick. But I blame the courts, the judges are too soft with them, don't punish them enough. They only have to tell the judge that they didn't have any toys to play with when they were kids and he lets them off. UGH!

☐ Life today is so fast, there isn't time to stop and spit, never mind enjoy yourself.

I Got Myself A Job

☐ I was left a ten bob widow when my husband died from a massive heart attack. I was absolutely devastated. One son was at university and my girl was in college. I was in limbo. At forty-nine I was too young to be a widow yet too old to retrain for work. It was a year before I did anything.

Then I got myself a job in a fancy goods shop. The people who owned it had a great sense of humour and helped me a lot. I must admit I didn't like the rubbish they sold but the owner realised that and used me like a gauge. If it was a beautiful ornament he went to buy and I liked it he would buy one. If it was an imitation sunflower with a face painted on and I told him it was totally tasteless, he'd buy a gross.

☐ I worked in a big haberdashery shop, worked up to manageress and had the biggest wage apart from the manager. Mind you working in shops taught us discipline, we couldn't go to work any old how, we had to have a uniform black dress. I could get a small discount on things but it was so small it didn't make much difference. I made many friends with the men and women customers. My husband worked in the same shop at one time, that's where I met him.

☐ I didn't like staying at home all day when I stopped being a dinner lady at school, so I got a job in a busy baker's shop — I can still smell that bread. But the owner was ever so keen with his money. Once I was three pence down in my till at the end of the day, he made ever such a commotion over that three pence — but he had to die and leave it in the end. He couldn't take it with him.

Women became carriage cleaners during the Great War

The railway station at the turn of the century. The taxi cabs were all horse drawn.

☐ It was just after the first war when women really started to emerge. The women's movement was all the rage. I was in agreement with them but I was never brave enough to take action and be force fed. I should have hated to have gone to prison for the women's movement. I used to go to political meetings in schools, both Labour and Conservative, although I leaned towards Labour because I used to lodge with a railway worker and his family who took the Daily Herald.

☐ I remember the horse drawn carriages in town and the Great Central Railway. I was unemployed with a green card for six years and then got a job at the plant and stayed there for another twenty-nine years. I worked on the Flying Scotsman and the Sir Nigel Gresley while they were under steam. I went to Liverpool with two fitters and lifting gear to help load the Flying Scotsman aboard ship for removal to America. When her buyer in America ran into financial problems, she was bought back by McAlpine and returned home.

☐ I worked on the railways and worked my way up to track chargeman then supervisor. I could have made chief inspector but didn't want that job. Well, you know, it would have meant lots of meetings and all that stuff.

☐ My father and grandad worked on the railways, I think it was in my dad's blood, he was a driver on the steam engines and was always known as driver Fred. Even after he finished work he was still a real railway man. My husband tried the railways but didn't really like it, one reason was the funny shifts.

☐ I've always had joy out of helping folk. They all used to fetch me when they needed help yet I never neighboured; I can't do with neighbours in and out of each other's houses. Deaths, miscarriages, broken legs they all came running to me. One woman came chucking pebbles at my window in the middle of the night. "Mrs Smith can you come?" she shouted. I put some trousers over my nightdress and forgot my teeth in the rush. It was always happening.

Locomotive works

The upper turnery of the railway plant in 1916

Spring shop at the locomotive works in 1948

Woodhouse, Osborne & Co. − brass finishers at Hexthorpe

☐ After leaving school, I went to learn dressmaking at Miss Leeson's in Capley Road. I went three months without being paid a penny, working 8am till 8pm; then I got one shilling a week for fifteen months. This was always put in a sealed envelope for me to give to my mother. After my training I received two shillings and sixpence each week, but then decided to do sewing work at home. I was afraid to charge for sundries though, so I didn't make much of a living at it. At nineteen I got a job in an office and stayed there till my retirement.

☐ Home was a three-up and three-down; one of the downstairs rooms was given over to the dressmaking business. We were apprentice dressmakers to Miss Spalton at Netherhall Road, Sunny Bar. Then my sister Muriel set up in business at home and I joined her. We had regular clients who stayed with us for years.

Our customers knew what they wanted and would come to us with a picture from a fashion book and we'd send for a pattern or adapt a pattern we already had and they supplied their own materials. I can remember when Silko thread was three ha'pence each or two bobbins for tuppence ha'penny. I still do a lot of sewing but now they're fifty-seven pence each. It's the same with dress patterns − they used to be half a crown and now they're anything from five to seven pounds.

The garments we made were machine sewn with hand finishing on the details. We'd finish about two outfits a week though it actually took about three weeks to make a garment because they needed a few fittings. The pay was very poor for all the hours that went into making clothes but I did it to help Muriel out as much as anything. Even after I got married, that would be 1931, I carried on working with Muriel, though after my sons were born I could only help out part-time. That was sixty-six years ago till she retired in 1975. We've always worked together and we've never fallen out.

☐ I worked as a core maker at Woodhouse's, which was a brass foundry, from being fourteen years old. I worked there about thirteen years and then worked for a while in catering before going back to Woodhouse's. After I married and had a son, I worked in the plant offices as a cleaner from 6am till 9am for five days a week. I also did Friday nights from 4.30 till 7.30. I retired from there at sixty-two and I've been full of aches and pains ever since. I wish I'd never given up work − I was always fit till then.

☐ I used to work in Balby laundry and then for seven years I worked in the laundry at Western Hospital, which at one time used to be a workhouse for down and outs. When my husband got a job in Stafford, we moved and I worked as a catering supervisor at the technical college there. I was turned sixty when I retired from there about twelve years ago but didn't come back to Doncaster till five years ago. It was after my husband died, and I still had friends and my son here in Doncaster so that's what brought me back.

☐ I'm eighty-nine tomorrow so I was born with the new century. Originally I came from Lincoln. I left school at fourteen and went to work as an apprentice in a millinery workroom in a shop. For the first year I worked without any pay at all but when I was twenty-two I came to Doncaster as head milliner for Dennis Roberts which was a large, well known business in Doncaster at the time. But after a few years he closed down so all the staff were served with their notice. I got a very good reference from them because I was a very good milliner so I got a job at Mexborough without any trouble.

I didn't stay there long because I didn't like the place much so then I went to work for Miss Pollock who had a classy millinery shop in Printing Office Street near the Co-op, at the time when the Co-op was lots of little separate shops. I worked for her until 1937 when she retired and she asked me if

The shop where I took over the millinery business from Miss Pollock − during the big freeze of '47

Coal delivery in the 50s from Denaby & Cadeby colliery

Bond Street corner shop

Hyde Park bus terminus in early 70s showing first phase of the Arndale Centre which is now called Frenchgate Centre

I'd like to take over the shop. I was fortunate in getting the business for nothing, I just bought the stock off her, and she allowed me to pay for that in small instalments.

Eventually I got notice from the Co-op that they were going to pull the place down and build the new emporium in its place, so I moved to a shop in Priory Place. There was just me, a lady and a girl working in the business and when the war started we had great difficulty in getting hold of the materials. About that time I was asked to do a talk for the Women's Institute and shortly afterwards asked if I'd run a night school class for millinery at the High School. The class became so popular that one night became two nights – and I was still running the business so I was kept very busy.

By the mid fifties the rent and rates on the property went up and up and the hat business started going down. Up until the fifties, you weren't dressed without a hat. Women wore a hat even if it was just to go down the street for a bottle of milk, and even now I wouldn't go out of the house without wearing a hat. But fashions change and women began wearing hats less and less. In 1956 I decided to give up the business but I didn't retire, I carried on teaching night school until I was well into my seventies.

☐ I was a nurse before I married and afterwards I carried on nursing part-time till I was sixty years old. It was private nursing that I did. I nursed sick and elderly people in their own homes. Before I was married, I'd be about twenty-six, I lived in at Doctor Bruce's house when his wife had her second baby.

Of course it was before the National Health started in 1948 but the people I nursed had money and private nursing was well paid even if it was hard earned. At least there was no housework or cleaning, they had other staff to do that. I particularly liked night nursing.

I would have liked to have specialised in midwifery. After I was married I was often called out to women in labour when they were unable to get hold of the midwife. But then she'd walk in when it was nearly over and get paid; I got nothing. I once delivered triplets when the mother thought she was only having twins. They gave me plenty of thanks but no money. Still, I enjoyed helping.

□ I'm eighty-three years old now and at one time everyone knew me round here; they always sent for me in times of need. I've handled miscarriages, broken legs and deaths, I've never refused giving help. I got a lot of joy doing things for other people.

□ The doctor used to lend me out for special events among his friends and I laid tables and waited on. I sometimes worked in the Mansion House in Doncaster High Street. I did enjoy the work.

I went into domestic service from leaving school. I loved working with high class people, serving with nice china in nice homes with high standards. I was taught service work by a cook to a gentleman farmer at Warmsworth. He lived in the front rooms and I lived in the back with the housekeeper. After that I went to work for the doctor.

My mother had spent time in service and taught me high standards. She was very strict and there was no dodging work, I learned to do things properly. I was just as strict with my own children.

I carried on working in service when I was first married. My husband used to work in the Staffordshire potteries and came to Edlington to work in the pits. I got to know him through my brothers who also worked at the pit. I was married at nineteen and carried on working in service till I was twenty-four and my son was born. Even then I worked on and off because they kept calling on me.

I also did other odd jobs; wallpapering and taking in sewing for friends, anything to earn extra money. But I drew the line at

Workers at the brass foundry

The Balby/Becket Road tram provided a cross-town service.

washing. I think everybody should do their own stinking washing.

The trouble with doing sewing in a small village — it was only plain things, boys' trousers, shirts, that sort of thing — was that I only got paid half the time. They'd send the kids to my door and they'd ask, "Have you finished me mam's sewing? If you have, can she have a look at it?" So I'd give it them to take and show their mothers and they'd come back and say, "Me mam says thanks and she'll settle with you later." Half the time they never did, and I didn't ask. I might eventually see the woman in the street and she'd say, "Oh sorry. I'd forgotten about the sewing — I'll send our lad round with the money." But she rarely did.

☐ At seventy-one I'm still working as a warden at some old people's houses. Nuttall's Mintoes built them for single women. The women I visit range from sixty-one years old to nearly ninety. The houses are near the racecourse and women have to have lived within a ten mile radius of Doncaster for at least twenty years to qualify. The warden before me was eighty-seven when she retired.

☐ At the turn of the century when I was a child, people often went to prayer meetings at four o'clock in the mornings. On Sundays the preachers were often out from dawn till dusk, travelling long distances to preach in the small villages.

My mother was asked to be caretaker of Hyde Park Primitive Methodist Chapel and we moved into the house attached to the premises about 1908. I continued as caretaker when it changed to the Church of the Prophesy though I worshipped at the Methodist new chapel. We were very involved in all chapel activities; Sunday School, Bright Hour, Christian Endeavour and Prayer Meetings. I was taught the piano and sang in the choir and when I was sixteen, I played the chapel organ for a service for the first time.

There was a wedding booked. The choir were there and the choirmaster was waiting for the minister to come. The bride came but the minister still didn't turn up so someone had to go and fetch him. He was shaving and he'd forgotten all about the wedding. By the time the minister arrived, the organist had to leave to go to work and asked me to play in his place.

☐　My grandmother never retired. It's difficult to compare her life with today's senior citizens. They are just worlds apart. She worked harder in the house than anybody doing a paid job. She was a tiny woman about four foot ten inches tall and a very timid, private sort of person. The only style of clothes she ever wore was a long black dress with a black apron on the top of it. Her hair was pulled back into a bun, she wore small oval wire rimmed glasses and looked exactly the same all her life.

For her, retirement was just a long continuation of the hard slog she had always known. This was because her two elder sons never married so they always lived at home. They worked in the pit, both took different shifts so she had to cook two dinners every day, one in the afternoon for the end of the morning shift and one for ten o'clock at night.

Bread making was a twice a week job. When she made the bread for the weekend she always put a handful of epsom salts into the mix because she said, "When the lads have been down the pit with all that dust all week, they need a good physic."

Then The Boss Gave Me A Clock

☐　When I retired from work as a greengrocer I thought I'd take life easy, especially as my workmates clubbed up and bought me an armchair and then the boss gave me a clock, a sort of glass domed thing with little brass balls swinging around. Well, after sitting for a full week in this chair watching the balls on the clock swinging I thought I'd go mad.

Still working as a knife mirror-polisher.

Stephen McClarence

24

A knife maker by trade, he retired 3 years ago at eighty-six

Stephen McClarence

☐ After I'd done twenty-five years at Crompton and Parkinson's foundry they presented me with a watch with an inscription on the back. I treasure that very much. Seven years later I retired and they gave me seventy pounds when I left.

☐ After I retired I got fed up with being on my own all day. My husband had died two years before so I got a job as an evening worker, they call it the twilight shift, at Peglar's. I worked two or three years and enjoyed it; well, it helped to take the lonely evenings away a bit. Then I met my new husband. We are both retired again now and we enjoy ourselves.

☐ At the moment life is very pleasant. I was pleased to retire and I'd been looking forward to it for some time. I felt I'd done my whack, especially the last three years.

From 1937 till 1941 I worked as an apprentice pharmacist and became qualified at the age of twenty-two. I went into the army through the war years. Well we didn't have any choice in the matter did we? Then after the war, I spent the next sixteen years working as a medical representative to all the doctors in Sheffield. The rules and regulations were very strict on drugs and I always say that you can't teach an old dog new tricks so four years ago I retired.

☐ I was widowed thirteen years ago. It was the same time that my sister retired from her business so we both made a break and were lucky enough to get flats near to each other, close to the Travis Garden Community Centre at Hexthorpe, so we can still enjoy each other's company regularly.

☐ After working forty-five years down the Denaby and Cadeby pits, suddenly I badly needed a hobby. It took me about twenty minutes to get used to the idea of not having to get up at four o'clock in the morning but quite a long time to settle down at home without work.

Still working as a mechanic.

Money Matters

☐ I got up early when I was sixty. I said, "I'm going down to that post office and I'm going to rattle on the door for my pension." I've had thirty years of pension out of them so far. You get an extra twenty-five pence once you pass eighty, you know, so next year I'll really be able to live it up.

☐ I used to have three allotments, my sons helped me with them a good bit and the vegetables and things I grew went a long way to helping out my pension. But then I went partially blind. I tried for a blind pension but found I would be five pounds worse off than with my old age pension, so I can't get any help moneywise with my loss of sight. I've had to give up my gardens because I can't manage them now.

I save for my bills, put a little bit away each week out of my pension. Mind you, I don't do too bad with the rebates I get.

☐ I think we pensioners are well done to and I can't see why people can't manage if they eat and live properly and don't waste their money. I think it's marvellous the way we are looked after. I don't know if that's universal though or just Doncaster Council who looks after us well.

My only grumble is that pensioners with money in the bank are penalised all the time. We never get a rise because it's given in one hand and taken from the other. I've never been able to claim for anything as I sold my house so I've got a bit of money at the back of me. Trouble is there's so many rules and regulations all tied up with red tape, my little red ball is always tied.

☐ There's not much we can do at this stage to improve our standard of living. What say do we have to make the government see what they are doing? No, it doesn't want a few old people protesting, it wants every living person in Great Britain to shout out. Everyone standing side by side in protest, because face it − old age comes to everyone if you live long enough.

☐ Of course there's less money now but that doesn't worry me as long as I can put a bit by for bills. I believe that one can build up a good full life without loads of money. All I do isn't very expensive and I'm happy and content. When I look back over my life I realise I have bags full of memories; no, I don't think I would swop any of it.

☐ When I draw my pension I always put five pounds away, it helps me to pay telephone and other bills. And I never skimp on food. I love my food and have a very sweet tooth but I've given my sweets up for Lent.

☐ The amazing thing about retirement is that I get paid for not working. All my life I've had to work hard for money. I get a good pension but we would be a lot better off moneywise if we didn't smoke. But apart from our cigarettes we spend very little on luxuries. I don't think we could manage on just the state pension but we'd scratch by if we had to.

☐ Since I retired from the pit six years ago, I got myself a little job as a cellarman at the local pub. It's only an hour every morning but it gives me a reason to get up and get started on the day. I also go round the local estate doing gardening and a bit of decorating for people I know. It's a good way of keeping active and making my pension go a lot further.

☐ I guess it is hard being a pensioner, not only being short of money but growing old as well. I try to keep my mind off my age; I go into Doncaster a lot and look round the shops and markets for hours without spending anything. I've got my bus pass so I might as well make use of it.

I live on my own but always take the trouble to cook myself a dinner even if it's just for myself. Well, I've got to eat haven't I? And I'm not helping anybody by neglecting myself. I buy the cheap cuts of meat but, you know, a bit of lamb neck done slowly in the oven can be very tasty.

☐ If I go into town I always go and have a look around the Age Concern shops. I pick up many a bargain there. I look after myself all right and can generally manage my money but the water rates and bigger bills are a trouble for me to pay. A bit more money wouldn't go amiss.

☐ It's a damn sight harder managing after retirement than it was before. I paid three or four pounds superannuation when I worked as a home help. I thought it would cover me for when I retired but now I have to pay full rent. I'm worse off for having paid it. When I want a new coat or dress I have to put so much away each week. Then you can't always get what you want because fashions don't cater for little old people.

I have to concentrate hard and channel my thoughts or I'd be bitter for the rest of my life. Pension money is only just enough to live on. It does make you bitter when you think you have another fifteen or twenty years to live. It's depressing as well. We organise jumble sales because we can't always afford new clothes. I have to pay the same for shoes as Thatcher does because nobody wants shoes second hand, do they? I'd like to go and see other places, theatres in London for instance, but I've never got enough. It makes you angry when you've always paid your dues — and our wages were never enough to save off.

☐ I don't really go short but I do have to cut back for things I want. You know, I was such a spendthrift when I was young and had plenty.

☐ Some folk never seem to learn how to manage money, they never have anything when they're earning good money, they spend it as it comes so if they're ever out of a job or on pension they're pleading poverty. Give them ten thousand pounds, they'll spend it on daft things while they've got it and then cry poverty again.

My daughter-in-law's like that. Money burns a hole in her pocket. She spends it on stupid things, things she doesn't need, but then her mother was just the same so it's no wonder she never learned any money sense.

Making ends meet

My son works hard and earns decent money but they've never got anything and she's always in debt. I've helped her out many times in the past but I wouldn't do it now even if I could afford to; she's nearly fifty so she's never going to change. God help them when they have to manage on pension.

☐ I cope better with bills since I retired than I did before. When you struggle on low money all your life, a pension isn't bad at all. I have a system in a plastic margarine box, I put so much away each week for television, electric, gas and insurance. I pay each bill as it comes and that's good management. I don't believe these folk who say they can't cope, they mustn't have a system.

☐ I draw my pension on Tuesday mornings so every Monday night I empty my purse and whatever's left in it I save in a box. Sometimes it might be as much as fifty pence, sometimes it's only a few coppers, but no matter how little, it goes in the box and it's surprising how it mounts up and helps to pay for those little luxuries. I learned that from my mother who always did the same. She used to say, "If I can get through the week without spending it, I can also manage without it the following week."

Of course managing your money is about having a budget. I can get by on only my pension because I've always had to get by on low money.

☐ No, we don't have as much money as when we were working but we cut back. Trouble is, the way the bills come through the letter box. Electric, gas, water, phone — they cost as much, if not more once you're retired. They're not switched off most of the time, like when you're out at work all day. I sometimes think I'll never have anything to call my own.

☐ My children don't realise how hard put to money we really are. They think we have a good carry on but they'll be in for a bit of a shock when anything happens to us because

there's no money and it's a council house. They are good kids but I don't believe in taking off them, it's not right. I can remember having to pay ten shillings a week to the Parish to help keep my parents and there were times when I couldn't afford it. We had some hard times finding that ten bob every week but it was compulsory, you see. I wouldn't want to put that kind of pressure on my kids.

I limit myself to two pints of beer on dance nights, that's the only time I go out now. I cut Sunday dinner drinking out, had to do to save for bills. At first I was too proud to go for a rent rebate but I had to do when they put the rent up another two pounds a week.

☐ I feel sorry for some of the pensioners. They haven't enough to live on. I used to take an old man his dinner every day or else he'd get nothing to eat. He had a houseful of old furniture, I wouldn't have had any of it given me but now that furniture would be worth a fortune.

☐ I've never worked — except in the house and bringing up the children, but we're both enjoying my husband's retirement. We've got less money coming in, of course, but the mortgage is paid and we no longer have the expense of running a car. We both have our hobbies, individual and shared, and we can still afford to smoke and enjoy a bottle of wine occasionally.

☐ Some old people talk a lot about the good old days but I think they were the bad old days; we're much better off and better looked after today. When I retired, the only income I had was my state pension but I'd saved a little bit of money while I was working so this helps pay for holidays and the little luxuries in life.

My father died when I was five years old so my mother was a widow for years and had to take in boarders to make ends meet. She met her second husband that way, he was one of her lodgers, but she never had the chance to retire. So when I compare my

Campaigning Pensioners

Stephen McClarence

Still running her general store

retirement with my mother's, I know how well off I am.

☐ I manage my money quite well, these slippers I've got on cost me fifteen pounds. The office in the home here at Shadyside buys them, then we pay for them out of our pension.

☐ You know you find your friends when poverty knocks on your door. A lot of people fail to understand the word poverty, it's only a small word but it can send you cold if you know the meaning of it. But I'm sure we'll always find that it's the poor that helps the poor. We have to make and take care of our own lives, don't we?

☐ I like to read but they get a lot of silly books in this home like Mills and Boon romances so I have to put up with those. They take our pension and then give us spending money. One week I get 8.20, the alternate week I get 8.30, I have my hair shampooed each week and that costs me two pounds, and I buy a lot of fruit.

☐ I can manage my money, but only just. I don't smoke and I'm not knocking those who do. If they enjoy a cig or a game of bingo, that's their pleasure but they shouldn't grumble if they don't have enough money left for other things.

Of course I have to cut back on little luxuries. I buy cheaper cuts of meat but I'll never be as mean as a woman I used to work for when I was in service as a young woman. She used to mark the loaf with a pencil and we weren't allowed to cut beyond the pencil line.

He makes rocking-horses for his grandchildren.

A Bit Of Fun And Frivolity

How Did I Ever Find Time To Work?

☐ I'm one of Thatcher's casualties. I was made redundant immediately following the miners' strike and at fifty-three I'd not much chance of getting another job so I took my redundancy and decided to make the best of my enforced retirement.

I swim three or four times a week at the local sports centre to keep fit and my garden and greenhouse keep me busy. My wife grows the flowers but I only believe in growing what I can eat. You can't beat a carrot or piece of cauli straight from the garden but I've had a go at growing a few exotic plants as well; bananas and kiwi fruit, I've grown them both in my greenhouse.

I grew the kiwi fruit from seed last year and it's now six feet high so I've just brought two proper plants to cross fertilise. It needs one male plant to six females. Then I might get some fruit off them. I've also got a grape vine going.

I saw this television programme about panning for gold in Scotland. When I was young, I once applied for a job in the Giant Yellowknife gold mines in Alaska. I even got offered the job but I didn't go because then I started courting Gladys. But I always had a fancy for goldmining so me and Gladys are planning on taking a tent up there and making a holiday of it. In the Grampians, just above Glasgow, it should be fun.

There's also a chap up in Scotland who grows fantastic crops and exotic plants by hydroponics so I'm planning on stopping by to see him while we're up there. Hydroponics is a method of keeping the plant roots in this circulating liquor full of nutrients and he gets about five times the amount of crops as he would by normal cultivation methods. He's on the same latitude as Moscow and he's able to grow tropical crops like bananas and kiwi fruit, so he might be able to give me a few tips.

I've also taken up genealogy recently. I'm trying to track down relatives in Canada and America. The family came from Burton-on-Trent originally and there's a place with Yoxall, my surname, in the midlands. I've found nothing so far in the church records so I'll probably go down to St Catherine's House in London later in the year if I don't have much success with local records.

You know, when I was working, I often did twelve hour shifts, seven days a week, but I'm not half enjoying my retirement now.

☐ A lot of old folk give in too easily once they retire. My husband thinks the same as me. He's had two heart attacks but every time he's poorly he says, "Don't give my garden up will you?"

I worked in a bookie's shop and played piano in a pub for years before I retired. Now I don't know how I ever found time to work. I exercise my daughter's dog — she's not as fit as me. I go dancing regularly and I go to the community centre three times a week.

☐ When my husband was getting near to retirement, we took up genealogy as a hobby because we'd always had a general interest in family history. We've traced my husband's family name of Pogmore back to 1750. We have information going back even further but there are a lot of gaps before then so there's no knowing for certain that it relates to our direct family line. Pogmore is a popular South Yorkshire name; there is a place near Barnsley called the same and an Adam de Pogmore going back to the 14th century.

We started with what we knew about the existing family and then searched back through parish registers, military records and census records. It is a really interesting hobby but not an expensive one. It doesn't usually cost much more than your time, although sometimes there is the cost of our fares when we go searching further afield. It's amazing how helpful people are when we're out and about trying to dig up information − and it's surprising what you find out.

My great-grandfather was a groom at Alderley Hall. He was kicked to death by a horse and the hoof from that very horse was passed down the family to us, though I don't know whether the horse was shot after killing my great-grandfather or died sometime afterwards. It would have depended how the family at Alderley Hall valued my great-grandfather against the horse.

My own family go back as far as the Huguenots who came over from France about 200 years ago. They were lacemakers, and I've taken up lacemaking myself; the inclination to try it came from a holiday at Le Puy in France, where my daughter-in-law comes from. The women there were sat in doorways, gossiping and lacemaking. It's a very complex skill but they were working with hundreds of bobbins at a time and made it look so easy as they sat chatting away.

The most adventurous thing I've attempted was a small mat. I worked it with sixty bobbins and it took all my concentration to avoid getting into a muddle with them. In fact it took me so long to make that mat that I certainly did not intend using it afterwards. My husband framed it for me instead and it now hangs on the wall. I prefer to do handkerchief corners, they're less complicated and don't take so long to do.

We once visited Honiton where there were only four original lacemakers left and there was a danger of the craft dying out altogether, but it seems to have gained a new popularity. A lot of people are taking it up now because it's such an interesting hobby. I also do knitting and tapestry work. I learn it at the same centre where my

I grow exotic plants from seeds I brought back from a holiday in Barbados

husband does his oil painting. We do a lot of things together now he's retired and it gives us a great deal of pleasure. We've always got on well and enjoyed each other's company.

Of course, I've never been so houseproud that the housework couldn't wait if something more interesting comes up, and now that my husband is retired, he shares the housework too.

☐ I spend most of my days drawing thatched cottages and villages. I've always dreamed of living in one. Never will now, so I draw them with felt pens, it keeps me busy. I'm seventy- seven years old but I don't feel it and I say you're as young as you feel.

☐ I read a bit. I like the Mills and Boon books, they help to take me out of myself. I like doing crosswords and I go into Doncaster to do my shopping. I used to go to Hexthorpe Flatts to hear the brass bands but there's nothing there now − it's a pity.

☐ Growing old is a rotten business but one we have to put up with and try to keep our hands and brain working. I have to keep busy, I can't just sit with nothing to do so I have my handiwork to keep me occupied − knitting, sewing and crochet. I've knitted a number of my own dresses, one is very full and pleated, I can't really wear it under a coat but it looks lovely for walking out in.

All my life I was involved with the Tory party, in my younger days I used to go canvassing but as I got older I just helped at functions to raise money for the party. We had whist drives and dances, I always enjoyed dancing.

I lived near the racecourse. I didn't go to race meetings but I went to exhibitions and shows, being retired I have time to do things like that.

☐ I've developed my own photographs. I still cut my own hair, I get lumps of it and snip. I like a quiff at the front. I've always liked dressing up. In my day people dressed dowdy once they passed forty but now old folk are quite well catered for in fashionable clothes. You can't tell how old they are these days.

☐ I went to a fortune teller, paid my shilling and waited. He came out almost fainting and said he couldn't do any more. He said he could feel all the pains of the previous person's mother, so I never got my shilling's worth. I've never been a believer in anything like that. I used to like going to see what they were up to, it made me giggly. Some of my more solemn friends thought I giggled too much, but I couldn't help it. I was once thrown out of a seance for laughing. I've always had a sense of the ridiculous.

☐ My hobby is writing. I'm never so happy as when I've got pen to paper. Since I've retired I have done more writing and joined a guitar class when my husband took it up. I'm a bit slow in learning and my fingers aren't very fast on the chords but it adds to my interest and helps me to make friends. I've also started keep fit classes, they are only gentle exercises but more important, I'm meeting other people.

☐ I tell people I live in a fantasy world. I like reading and I've read all of Catherine Cookson's books. If it wasn't for television and the library I don't know what I should do. But I need my own little castle so to speak. I'm never really lonely and I've got good neighbours either side of me but we don't run in and out of each other's homes.

I've been widowed for eleven years but at eighty-odd it's a bit late to start rebuilding. I keep myself busy enough, though. If anything needs stitching I do it straight-away. My grandson, who I looked after when he was a baby, comes to see me every fortnight. I like to go down town during the day and I always meet somebody I know. My biggest love is plants and flowers, I take all my own cuttings and every window bottom is full of plants. I also play patience every day to keep my brain going. To me

She became a well know local writer in her sixties

I loved dressing up and still do

that's important because I wouldn't like to finish up somewhere like the Marshalls and end up sat in a chair looking vacant. I hope that never happens to me.

I don't bother going out drinking, I've always been more interested in putting food on the table. I can't stand the noise of clubs, turns and bingo – I can't stand bingo. I always have a glass of beer with my Sunday dinner; it's a tradition because I always used to go for a jug of beer when my husband was living so I carry on now.

☐ I'd like my paintings to go to good homes when I go to a better land because now I am eighty-nine, I know my time is getting near. I know I'm not going to get better and I know I'm not even going to improve. Yes, I'll soon be gone now and I'll thank God when it's time.

I'm a copyist. I decided at the age of seventy that I would like to paint, so with a friend I went along to Oswin Avenue night school in Balby. I've painted Lands End,

York Cathedral and several others. I did this with quite some success until I was eighty years old. I even had a write up about my paintings in the newspaper but I've had to give it up because of the arthritis in my arms, I can hardly lift them now.

I still have a lot of other interests; I keep my brain ticking over, I read quite a lot of books from the library and watch some television. But I hate this growing old bit, the worst part of it is not being very active now and the not being able to do such a lot of things.

I like to do the quickie crossword in the Daily Mail, it keeps me ticking over, my eyes are going, though. I looked at a clue and saw 'cruel' try as I might I couldn't fit anything. Next day I looked at the answer, 'skilly' it said. I wondered what that had to do with it but when I looked in the dictionary it said 'gruel'.

☐ We read a lot in winter now we're retired so we both joined Doncaster library.

I started learning the guitar at sixty-three

My husband likes detective thrillers, I'm a bit soft, I like romantic stuff like Barbara Cartland — you're never too old to dream.

☐   I have a garden but being no Percy Thrower I couldn't imagine spending my life in it after I retired so I started making wine and beer — not the kit stuff, though.

Then me and my wife got involved with the church and I read quite a lot of bible and joined fellowship groups. Through these I met many more new friends. Then I was asked if I would join the worship group and though I'm no aspiring tenor I enjoy singing with them at Sunday services.

They started running guitar classes, I was sixty-three years old at the time and when I told my wife I was going to join, she laughed. Nevertheless I bought a guitar from one of my grandsons and soon knocked a few chords off with it. This created a great new interest for me and I practised a lot. Now I play in the music group at some of the Sunday services which also involves one evening a week practising with them.

Recently I met a young couple who are members of the Conisbrough Light Opera Company and they asked me if I'd like to join them. I'm now looking forward to my first performance in *Guys and Dolls,* and although it's only a small part this means another practice night each week. So what with wine making, gardening, guitar lessons, singing, study groups, as well as hospital visiting, I have a very full life — in fact, I'm busier now than when I was working. But that's how I like it, I haven't time to get bored. I reckon nothing to sitting in an armchair with the newspapers all day. Plenty of time for that when I can't get about.

That's the secret of retirement and growing old happy. Never to be too old for a bit of fun. I also like to dance now and then.

☐   I used to do a lot of things; peg rugs and hookie rugs, crochet and knitting, but I can't do much with my hands now. I've still got a pegged rug I made. It has a black background and red roses on it and it's still on the floor after thirty years.

Santa Clause tempting Eve

Feeding the ducks

38

Doing a bit of gardening

After I retired I developed an interest in palmistry. Mind you, I'd always been fascinated by that sort of thing but I won't say that I took it seriously. So it started out as a bit of a joke when I went to see this palmist with a friend and I read a few books on the subject. You know the sort of things, about how to read the lines on your hand and I practised on my friends. It started out as a laugh but, sometimes, when I looked at people's hands, things just sort of popped into my head and when I told them, they surprised me by saying how accurate it was.

Of course, at first I put it down to knowing them well so I thought I'd just dug something out of my subconscious that they'd told me at some time, or seemed in keeping with the person they were. But then they started asking if they could bring friends along for me to have a go at reading their hands.

People I'd never met before said they were amazed at how good I was; sometimes they'd get in touch with me weeks or months after, saying that what I'd predicted had come true. It just grew from there. I was seeing so many people, I decided to make a small charge, just to earn a bit of money, seeing as I was spending so much time doing it. I've got people phoning up for appointments with me from all over now. Some come from as far as Leeds. It's almost a full time job with me now and since my husband died, at least I don't have to manage on just a pension.

My friend took up dried flower arranging when she retired. She didn't go to any classes, she taught herself but she does these fantastic arrangements and has started a good little business. She can sell everything she makes, her work is in such demand. She also makes pictures and birthday cards out of pressed flowers. She regularly goes round craft fairs to sell her arrangements and has been to some fairs where all the stall holders dress up in period clothes. She really enjoys the dressing up ones.

☐ My chief interest was photography so I joined a camera club. I started off with a Box Brownie which cost me twelve shillings and sixpence and I made my first enlarger out of a soap box, with the help of my father. Later I was delighted to win the Jordan Rose Bowl Trophy, which was presented by Fred Jordan, a well known Doncaster solicitor and President of the camera club for many years. I also won a one pound voucher for a picture published in the Doncaster Gazette entitled 'The valley of the Don'. It was taken from Sprotborough Bridge.

☐ Since my husband retired we go for long walks through the countryside. We've also done a lot of dancing, ballroom that is. I always wore lovely dresses and did many demonstrations on dancing.

☐ My neighbour's led a really busy life since he retired. He joined an art club and has had some of his paintings in a local exhibition. He's built this huge conservatory on the back of his house which he uses as a studio and he built an extension to his garage so he can get all his woodworking equipment in the back because he's really gone into woodwork in a big way as well. He makes the frames for his pictures and all sorts of other things. I'm not sure exactly what, but he certainly does a lot of knocking and banging. He also ties his own flies for when he goes fishing, and he's taken up photography. He only retired 18 months ago so he's not suffering from boredom in his retirement. In fact he often says, "I don't know how I ever found time to go to work."

☐ My wife died three years ago and my daughter decided I needed a hobby to occupy my mind, so she bought me this matchstick model kit of a windmill. I phoned her up three hours later to tell her I'd finished it. Since then I've made all sorts of things out of matchsticks. My wife was ill

Matchstick model making

They run dancing classes for pensioners

Stephen McClarence

for some time, she was right poorly and I was looking after her twenty-four hours a day so I'd no time for anything else. But when she died, I'd suddenly all the time in the world.

After I'd done the model windmill, I didn't use any more kits, instead I drew my own design on a piece of paper and bought a large bag of unused matchsticks from a model shop. I glue the matches onto the drawing on the paper and then paint and assemble the model. I started off with fairly simple ideas and gradually progressed to more complicated ones. I've made an old fashioned Gypsy caravan, circus wagons with model animals inside, a cigarette box, Davy lamps that I've fixed up with a light inside and birdcages with ornamental birds in them. I've used ordinary, burnt matches for some models. I did an eagle mounted on a mirror and the burnt match ends give a better effect of feather tips. I've given a lot of my models away to neighbours and people in the village and the old ladies

round here save me their broken beads and other bits and pieces that come in useful for decorating some of the models.

I've been working on a model fairground for the past eighteen months and there'll be another six to eight months' work before it's completed. I've made the base and the big wheel, flying chairs and swing boats and a roundabout. I'm working on the cocks and hens at the moment, trying to fix in a crankshaft so they'll move up and down as they go round. There's the hoopla and the roll-a-penny stalls to do yet. I intend to put in motors so they will be working models and I've experimented with an old electric razor which makes the flying chairs turn.

I've always been good with my hands, I used to do a lot of fretwork when I was younger. I'd get an old tea chest and make toys for all the kids in the village when it was coming up to Christmas – doll's houses, kicking horses, all sorts of things. I work about thirty hours a week on my models and I'm a lot better for having this hobby. It requires my full concentration while I'm doing it because it's very fiddly and precise work, so it doesn't leave me with much time to feel lonely or brood on my problems.

☐ My sister and I are both keen knitters and sewers, still make our own clothes, dresses, petticoats and nightdresses. Alice is keen on house plants, she has them all over the flat. I took up a new hobby when I retired from dressmaking, I took up cake making. I didn't have any time for hobbies or interests while I was working but I have this special recipe, it was in some papers from Sainsbury's and it's a beautiful fruitcake. Alice has always been a good cake decorator so now I make the fruitcake and she decorates it. They are lovely cakes and sometimes we make one for the raffle at the Community Centre. The money from the raffles goes into the funds towards trips and outings.

☐ I used to have very active hobbies; hockey, tennis and dancing at the Dunlop Sports Centre in Birmingham. But at seventy years old my hobbies are more or less restricted to watching television and reading the papers. I like to do the crosswords but those page three girls showing their bare boobies put me off. Some look like spaniels' ears drooping.

☐ Three years ago I had a collapse and was taken in to Tickhill Road Hospital. I was ninety at the time and I had just been doing too much. I wasn't there long before I was moved to Conisbrough Hospital and was there until I came to this old people's home two years ago. When I was at Conisbrough I used to go to a day centre once a week and it was there that I took up painting because one of the helpers was interested in painting. I'd done painting in watercolours and oils as a child and hadn't done any since but now I've taken up watercolour painting again.

☐ Bernard's retirement was early and quickly decided upon so it took some time

Still painting in her nineties

Horseshoe Pond was the terminus for the racecourse tram

to adjust. But he very soon filled his time with many voluntary jobs for friends and neighbours and our church. We are both keen members of Doncaster Choral Society.

☐ I go to St James' Church where we have a lot of different functions; Mothers' Union parties, have tea, play bingo and help keep the church clean. We go to the vicarage and the vicar gives us a drink of sherry while we have discussions. We went on a trip to Sheffield to another church where we had a concert and we go to Hexthorpe church for social functions as well. The church people are very good to me.

☐ I hadn't been swimming for thirty years until I was tempted into a nice warm pool on holiday. All those years ago two lengths was about my limit. Today I managed twenty-two lengths at Armthorpe baths.

This Sporting Life

☐ I love a bit of fun and frivolity, it's what life is all about really. Now I like to go walking and I like to go for a pint. I like a bet on the horses, especially if the race is on television. Piggott was my favourite jockey, he was great, and my favourite wrestler is Mick McManus.

☐ I've always had an interest in sport, particularly horse racing. I go to York a lot to see the horses running especially now I've more time — and I always take my binoculars that my mates bought me for a retirement present.

☐ Remember the old Horseshoe Pond? It was where the racecourse roundabout is today. Any bent bookies that couldn't pay out at the races were dunked. Lots of outsiders would move in for race days, fleecing the crowds with crooked card games and taking their wages.

☐ Horse drawn Gypsy caravans used to arrive for Race Week. It was always the first week in September and ran from the Tuesday through till Friday. This would be the last week of the school holidays and 'the plant' always shut down for the week even though the workers didn't get paid for their time off. Many young couples chose to get married Race Week so they would be able to go away while the plant was closed.

One wedding photograph in the window of Don Studio had the bride and groom accompanied apparently by a red Indian. This was one of Doncaster Race Week's characters. He was known as Prince Monolulu and seemed to be of West Indian extraction and always turned up for Race Week wearing a huge brightly coloured Indian feathered headdress. He would appear at the old market top, (on top of the ice works where the market produce was kept chilled) and would shout, "I've got an 'orse." He was a tipster and sold tips to his customers, written on little pieces of paper.

I remember very early morning cycle rides with my dad. From Kirk Sandall to Doncaster we cycled to see the race horses have their early morning gallops. Prince Monolulu was always there to watch them exercise.

A big fair was held behind the Corn Exchange during Race Week. The Corn Exchange was also the venue for musical events staged by Mr Lawrence Harrison during the twenties. Famous guests from all over the world performed there including Paul Robeson. Mr Harrison himself was an accomplished baritone and his wife Annie a well known pianist.

☐ The sun was streaming down already and it was only eight o'clock in the morning. It was going to be a grand day and me and John Parkinson were larking about in the yard behind our houses. There was a great hum of excitement going round because a lot of the adults were going off to the races. It was the day of the St Leger.

I suppose we got caught up in the excitement and thought we'd go as well. I was ten, John was only eight but we were

Kings Entrance at the racecourse facing Grandstand Road, led directly into the Royal Box. It was demolished late 60s

On the way to a race meeting

good friends. So we decided to just follow the crowds. It seemed an awful long way from South Elmsall but we managed to grab a few lifts by standing on the backs of various passing vehicles. There were loads of folk on their way to the races and we were given pennies and ha'pennies on the way. We'd no shoes on so we were glad when we arrived.

It was the year Nighthawk won the St Leger but we didn't see a thing, it was so crowded and we were so small. So we collected as many butterscotch boxes as we could. They were wooden in those days and we thought the extra firewood might help square things back home. Wood was always welcome and we knew we were sure to be in trouble by the time we got back.

We were just about to set off back home when a policeman stopped us. "What are you two doing then?" he asked. It was the first time we'd felt scared throughout our great adventure. He carted us off to the Salvation Army where we had to stay overnight.

Next morning we were both given a pair of shoes and put on the train at Carcroft and sent back to South Elmsall. I still remember the good hiding that was waiting for us when we got home.

Getting Out And About

☐ I try to keep a young outlook myself. Old folk should stay active and by joining clubs, getting out and mixing with everybody, you don't allow yourself to get pushed to one side and forgotten about. I still go dancing regularly, old time and modern sequence. When you come to the centre as a 'young' pensioner you'd be surprised how fit some of the 'old' pensioners are. I'm going to keep active for as long as I can.

I'm currently on the committee of the community centre but it will soon be our AGM, and then of course they will vote for a new committee but if I'm voted on again I'll accept without hesitation − I've enjoyed doing it so much.

Donkey riding in Spain

Away from it all

☐ I like a drink and I'm a life member of the Doncaster Great War Comrades Social Club. I went for a holiday with them for three weeks to Redcar. I also get a book of tickets that enables me to get a pint of beer fourpence cheaper. I've got loads of happy memories but gave all my stuff that was worth anything away to my family.

☐ I didn't want to hurt my mates' feelings by not using the chair they'd bought me as a retirement present so I joined the library and sat in it to read. I learned more about old Henry VIII and his carryings on than enough, but I soon got bored with reading and being in the house all the time. Mind you, I help round the house a lot. The wife says I'm magic with the Hoover but I won't have dusting or window cleaning.

Then I got hold of a book Victor Sylvester wrote, it was about dancing, so me and my wife went to a working men's club and started to learn modern sequence dancing.

We used to row like hell when we first started, many is the time she's walked off the floor and left me, but now it's great. What I like about it is that there are new dances coming in every week, some of them from London. We've made lots of friends and went on holiday with other dancing partners. We had a week at Blackpool dancing in the Tower Ballroom. This has helped keep me young in heart, so to speak.

☐ I keep busy in lots of ways. Since my wife died I've become a fair cook and I do my own shopping and washing. I'm seventy-three but I can look after myself all right. Mondays, Wednesdays and Saturdays I go to the local community centre and sometimes I shout the bingo numbers for the women on Thursdays but I find Sunday is the worst day of the week. I go out to the local club but it still seems such a long day. I don't know why, I mean once you've retired, most of the days are pretty much the same but Sunday has an atmosphere and a feel all of its own.

☐ My sister and I always make a point of going out somewhere every day, even if it's only to visit each other. There's a lot of elderly people who don't get out from one week end to the next and it's too easy to get into the habit of not bothering.

☐ I joined the ladies' section of the Doncaster Chamber of Commerce before I retired from business and eventually became Chairman. After I'd retired and had more time, I joined the Townswomen's Guild. It was about 1956 when the Doncaster branch had just started, then I joined the Balby branch because it was more local. I was treasurer for seven years and then I became chairman for a year. Unfortunately the Balby branch closed in 1988 due to lack of support. Today's young women are not joining, they have other things to do, which is a great pity. The Guild began soon after women got the vote and was intended for the betterment of women, but now they've got the vote, a lot of women don't bother to use it.

☐ Travis Garden Community Centre at Hexthorpe is a marvellous centre. The subscription is only fifty pence a year and for the past five years they've organised an outing to the Earl of Doncaster for Christmas dinner and we have parties New Year's Eve and Easter and we have bingo Thursdays and Saturdays besides dominoes and other table games.

We're kept ever so busy; running raffles, holding coffee mornings and we bring clothes in that we don't want and they go on a rail to be sold at tenpence each. All the money we raise is banked by our treasurer and then we have a share out and it helps to pay fares and things when we go on outings and holidays. We do have some fun, everyone is very lively and we always manage to get a full bus for the Cleethorpes trip but not so many fancy going up to the

I was President of Doncaster Chamber of Trade — ladies' section.

Enjoying a bit of sun

Dales. There are forty-two of us going to the Isle of Wight in April. Well, why not live it up while we can?

I've Travelled All Over The Place

☐ One of the pleasures of retirement is holidays out of season. They're much cheaper and there's no rowdiness.

☐ My husband Reg has stopped driving since he retired so now we use the twerlies to get about. Twerlies — those are the pensioners' bus passes, so called because if we try to use them before nine o'clock in the morning, the bus driver says, "Sorry, you're tw'early so you'll have to pay full fare."

I never learned to drive. I once started learning, we'd been married about twelve years when Reg started teaching me. And do you know, it was the first time in all our married life that he swore at me. Well, I wasn't standing for that and I packed in

driving there and then! But I've always regretted that I didn't stick with it.

☐ I've been on more holidays since my husband died than ever. I went to London on my own when I was in my late seventies. It only cost forty-nine pounds. My daughter went mad when I told her. She said, "For forty-nine pounds they'll put you in a wheelbarrow, run you down the M1 and leave you in a Salvation Army hostel."
Isle of Man. I met a lovely man there, he'd just lost his wife, he was a perfect gentleman. We went for long walks after dinner all over the island. We walked that island round the TT track. Then I went to Jersey. I'd never been in an aeroplane so I wanted to try it, we flew from Bournemouth. You're only in the air for an hour but it was lovely. A woman asked me if I'd flown before. When I said no, she said, "You might be sick. Take a barley sugar and don't look through the port hole." I ignored her, had a brandy and Canada Dry, looked

A trip to Oslo just after I retired

A coach trip to Brid

Ready to go on holiday

through the window and enjoyed every minute.

☐ I like to travel. I get sixteen railway passes a year because my husband worked on the railway before he died, so I travel a good bit with them. I've a son in North Wales and a cousin in Hemel Hempstead and I've been to Rome three times. I tried it first with a broken arm and twice since without. My brother says I'll never die in my own bed.

☐ I still have a car and we always make a point of having a day out somewhere each week, depending on what we fancy; sometimes to the coast, sometimes to the Dales and sometimes to one of the cities like York. We do it midweek, it's easier for parking and not so crushed.

☐ I go to Australia as often as I can to stay with my son and his family. I once went to an exhibition in Brisbane while I was there and did so much walking about the first day, I got very tired. The second day they got me a wheelchair and I was very glad of it but thank God there wasn't anyone there who knew me. Last time I went to Australia I had to go into hospital and the nurses said they just loved to hear me speak. I suppose I sounded strange to them.

☐ I'm still enjoying my life as much now at seventy-two as when I was younger. I keep myself healthy. I drink a bit, play a bit, and sleep a night well. I've been to Canada four times to visit my daughter, and to America and the Rocky Mountains.

I'd never been overseas before but since I retired I've travelled all over the place. I've been to Austria, Spain, Holland and I'm going to the Isle of Wight soon. My husband doesn't go, he likes his drink. It used to bother me but now it doesn't, I let him get on with it and I enjoy myself.

☐ I visited a lot of countries after I

Flying high in Switzerland.

retired. I will never forget my first morning in Switzerland, I went to the bedroom window opened the shutters and just stood there in awe, the sun was coming up over the mountains and it was beautiful.

I've always had that kind of nosey nature and have kept it up since I retired so when I went to Madrid I wanted to go to a bull fight but nobody would go with me. They say it's cruel, but I'm nosey and I wanted to see what they did, though I didn't really want to see them kill a bull.

☐ There's lots of old folk around me and no end of them go abroad or to the coast in the winter. Sometimes it's Spain, sometimes it's Yarmouth for Christmas. Often a large group of them go together − they swear by Wallace Arnold.

A couple of years ago − it might have been a trend, it might have been because of that bad winter − but they went for a month. Three hundred pounds for flights, accommodation and half board all thrown in. They reckon it was cheaper than spending the winter at home with the cost of heating and the rest.

☐ My husband worked on the railway, so I got a free travel pass and I've been all over the place − Scotland, Ireland and down to the South of England. I once went on holiday to Spain, but I caught Spanish flu, so that put me off ever going abroad again.

☐ We have done a bit of travelling since we retired. It's nice you know doing things together, but that doesn't mean we don't have rows because we do, proper ding-dongs at times. But we do enjoy holidays, we went to Salu then we went to Benidorm. We stayed in an apartment in Benidorm instead of an hotel and found it wasn't much dearer to stay for a month than a fortnight.

We bought quite a few meals out but one night I was tired so I sent my husband to a small take away cafe for chicken and chips twice and he came back with two whole chickens and chips, we were eating chicken all week. Then we found a cafe that sold pork and chips but I didn't send him for any, I thought he might come back with a couple of pigs and chips.

In February 1988 we went to Israel and toured the Holy Land. It was great but the weather wasn't too good, you see it's their winter the same as ours, though it was a bit warmer, but Jerusalem is so built up you always seem to be in the shade.

I was a bit worried about going as the PLO and Israel were fighting at the time, but apart from seeing armed troops walking about we didn't see any actual trouble, other than a shop being set on fire one night. But talk about the Irish, they've nothing on the Arabs; all the Arab shopkeepers were on strike so they closed and shuttered their shops at midday. If we wanted anything we went round to the back and they'd let us in. I went in one and the people were nearly stood on each other's heads it was that full.

☐ My wife and I enjoy our annual holiday. We go abroad every year to Italy, Greece, Spain or somewhere like that. We used to go down south to Torquay and around there but we find it's just as dear as going abroad now.

☐ We've been abroad a few times but the heat is too much for us so we bought a second hand car and caravan and hope to go touring through England, not bothered for Scotland though − it's always raining up there.

☐ Four years ago members of our community centre went to Amsterdam and visited the bulb fields. In '86 we went to Arnheim. We went by coach and went across the Channel on the ferry and stayed on a cruiser for a week and different visits to places of interest were included. It's all organised by the centre and the cost is reasonable. I'm able to save up and pay for the holidays out of my pension.

☐ I've gone on Saga Tours a few times. They're linked with Age Concern, you go there to book your holidays and of course you have to be over sixty. I've been to Guernsey, Portugal, Benidorm and Tunisia with them. One of the benefits is that a trained nurse always accompanies the tours, which is a good job because when we went to Tunisia in '82, cholera broke out in our hotel. Fortunately we'd all had injections before we went but they did tests all the same to make sure we were clear. Two people on our tour went down with severe diarrhoea though I'm not sure whether it was actually cholera or not. But one woman's husband died while we were there as well.

We've had some laughs on these holidays but the Tunisia one — well, I wouldn't go there again. We went for a fortnight and it was two weeks too long. It was jinxed from the start.

Apart from the cholera and the dead man, a woman had a large diamond ring stolen. Of course she should have put it in the hotel safe but she didn't, and it was stolen when she had a tray brought up to her room. She was able to identify the man who

took it; he was the only blue eyed Arab who worked there. And the camels were horrible flea-bitten things and were all over the beach. What with them and the police on horseback you couldn't lay down for animals.

I've never seen so many beggars, cripples, mosquitoes and flies. We went on a trip to the President's palace. It was full of gold inside and the outside was covered in beggars. Then we went to Hannibal's Palace, everywhere was marble, there was this fantastic pool with a bar in the middle. It was the place where millionaires stay so we had a sample of the good life for a few hours.

There was one beggar woman we saw regularly, she had no legs and she was always rocking a baby who was suckling at her breast. We'd give her all our odd coins when we saw her but she used to play hell about the coins. Presumably they were not worth enough. Then one day we watched her get up and walk away. We also saw tiny kids painting pottery for souvenirs for tourists. There was terrible poverty

High flyer

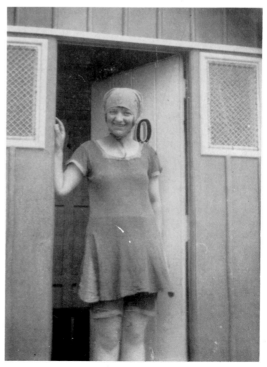

Going for a swim

We go on lots of trips

We've been to the zoo

Christmas party at The Marshalls

everywhere we went. Whatever we might think of the health service and pensions in England, it makes you grateful - though from the state of them, probably most of them don't live long enough to need a pension.

I didn't eat any of the food the hotel served up; octopus, saffron potatoes, bread like grey concrete. I only ate yoghurt. And the water was terrible, it wasn't fit to drink. I'd taken some biscuits from England thinking at least I'd be able to eat those but I put them in the wardrobe and the next time I got them out they were all nibbled. We sent for the manager to get rid of the mouse and they took the wardrobe apart and cemented up a hole in the wall, saying that that would cure the problem, but the next time my friend went to the bathroom the mouse was sat in the middle of the floor. Fortunately she didn't tell me that till we were on the plane going home, thank God.

☐ I've travelled all over England from Land's End to John O'Groats, and all the countries in Europe; Paris twice, Austria, Germany, Monaco, Switzerland, Spain, Italy and Holland and most of them by Sheffield United Tours. My travels started just before I retired and I've carried on travelling for the past twenty-odd years. My last trip was a few years ago when I was eighty.

☐ After Dad retired, him and my mother took their first trip abroad. They flew to New York where there's a branch of the family; about thirty cousins, aunts, uncles and the rest who we've never met and they intended visiting as many as possible. As they were getting near their destination, Dad did what he always did when they went on coach trips. He went round with his hat and had a collection for the pilot.

Companionship

You Can Take Your Memories Into A Bungalow

All The Family I Need

☐ I never married and I never wanted to. Perhaps I never met the right man but I had my own home and I could do what I wanted and go where I wanted. During the war a young woman with two children were evacuated from London and came to stay with me. After the war she stayed on because her husband was in the ambulance service and was killed in an air raid. She stayed with me until she died in the sixties and the children stayed until they grew up.

They still live in the area and come to see me often, so I had all the advantages of being married and have all the family I need, but none of the disadvantages.

☐ I've got all the romance in my life that I need. I've been married forty-three years, I don't know how I would cope if he died, but I don't think I would sit down and mope. Grieve, yes – mope, no. I would go all out to rebuild my life though I know I would never be able to replace my man.

☐ I've been on my own for twenty-eight years. My husband worked at the railway plant and one day complained about a pain in his chest. He went to work and dropped down dead. I'll never forget it. He'd always been a fit healthy man. I bought him a bottle of medicine and I remember him laughing and joking about it being the first bottle he'd ever had. He took a swig at dinnertime, got on his bike for work and I never saw him again.

I suppose the things I treasure most from my life are the fun times with my husband and children. My husband was digging his garden once and lost his watch, he never did find it, but he used to keep going out to look for the time. He'd spend hours with his mate sat on a plank across two buckets putting the world to rights. Then with the world all right

for another day he'd come in. No gardening done but everything was rosy.

I'm still alone now but I'm never lonely. I had a good marriage while it lasted but I wouldn't marry again. I couldn't do it, I would be comparing any man with my first.

☐ I retired from Bullcroft pit at sixty-five years old. My father was killed at the same pit in an accident – his arm was pulled right out. My brother Edgar is the manager of Rossington pit and he and his family come and visit me regularly. I never married so they're all the family I've got now.

☐ I was married forty-five years when my husband left me. I was watching television one evening when he came downstairs with his bags packed. We'd had no argument, there was no apparent reason for him to leave, but he walked out of the house and didn't come back. Well, he did ask if he could come back eventually but by then I'd moved into a one bedroomed flat and we'd been separated a few months so I didn't want him back.

We've been separated five years now and I've no regrets. In fact I wish I'd never got married in the first place. I trained as a nurse and and after a couple of years married realised that I would have preferred a nursing career to marriage. We didn't have a lot in common. I was a keen ballroom dancer but he wasn't. He wouldn't go on holiday so I didn't and he had no hobbies so particularly after he retired, he was under my feet all day.

His idea of retirement was to put on his slippers, put his feet up and watch telly. But just because you've retired is no reason to give up living and get old. So once I'd got used to the idea of him going I was happier without him.

☐ Loneliness is the main enemy of older

people. Companionship is very important, nobody should have to live on their own. Once you get past sixty, though, there aren't many men about.

☐ My wife agrees that if ever I come back in another life, I should come back as a Muslim. That way I could have four wives. One to wash and clean, one to cook, one to take out and one to take to bed. Being retired has made me sexier. I go swimming regularly, I get plenty of exercise so I'm much fitter and I've got more energy and inclination. Pity my wife doesn't feel the same.

☐ We had a good marriage. I've been a widow ten years now; he died at home from the 'miners' disease'. He used to call me Mam. He'd say, "If it suits you, Mam, it suits me." If the kids wanted anything he used to say, "Ask your Mam." We rarely disagreed.

He didn't do much in the house but that didn't matter, I was good at that. He was called Charles Henry but I always called him Harry. He liked to go for a drink, he wasn't a great drinker but most miners like a drink, I suppose it washes the dust down and sometimes I'd go down and join him. "I do love you, Mam," he said as he died.

☐ All my life I have treasured my memories of my first husband, Billy. He died of cancer just after his thirty-second birthday. He left me with three children but before he died he told me to get wed again so that the kids could have a father. Some time after, one of Billy's friends asked me to marry him. Before I agreed I made one condition, it was that Billy's photo should be left out all the time. I treasure that photo and those memories - he was very special. I think the first one always is.

☐ I was the youngest of four children and our family was what they call an extended one. Mother was one of twelve and father was one of seventeen. If aunts, uncles and cousins were ever counted the final total

Band of Hope demonstration in 1916

Over the wall

would be impressive. We always had a full house because times were hard and relatives were our only security in the so-called 'good old days'. If and when we had cake it was the windmill variety — if it goes round you get a bit. I laugh whenever I hear Val Doonican sing *Sleeping At The Foot Of The Bed*. Being the youngest and smallest I was often relegated there when we were overcrowded and I know exactly what he means.

☐   I nursed my mother till she died at eighty-three. I was in my early sixties then and it left me with a big gap in my life.

My mother suffered terribly. She used to ask, "Why doesn't the Lord take me?" When she died I wanted her back. I would have done anything to keep her longer. I suppose it was really selfish of me, when she was in so much pain. I wouldn't want anybody to have to do for me what I had to do for my mother but I enjoyed doing it all the same. I was on my own and it helped me.

☐   I got fifteen shillings a week when my husband died and an extra five shillings for my lad. He was eleven when his dad died. I went out cleaning so that I could look after him properly. He stayed with me till he was twenty-one and then the army took him for National Service. He did his two years and came back to me, he was never the same lad after that. I came home one day and found him with his head in the gas oven. I've had more than my fair share of tragedy in my life.

☐   There's this elderly couple live near me who go down to bingo a couple of times a week. They play for odds and sods, most of the prizes are donated, so I often see them coming up the street with a bag of sugar or half a pound of butter.

This chap's wife is always walking about two yards behind him and even if they stop to talk to somebody, as soon as they set off again, there he is in front and her bringing up the rear like Indian chief and squaw. It fascinates me because it's not as if he walks faster than her or she walks slower, otherwise she'd end up trailing miles behind him. But no, she just trundles steadily behind with just a couple of yards separating them. Presumably they have nothing to say to each other.

☐ My father was killed in France, at the battle of Verdun in the first World War, so my mother gave me Verdun as my middle name.

☐ I have never married, never found a man who I could share my life with. You know I wasn't cut out to be a housewife or mother. I look at the youth today and wonder what went wrong. Oh my goodness how they carry on. And they're so selfish.

I don't like children much. Being a spinster has been good. I was one of six kids and my mother had four children in less than four years. Well, what sort of life is that for a woman? It certainly put me off marriage and kids. I've got plenty of nephews and nieces though. I've a nephew lives in Harrogate and phones from time to time to say they're coming over for a visit and I've a niece in Scunthorpe who just drops in without any warning. When she does that we get fish and chips from the nearby chip shop so I don't need to bother getting a meal. The others live further away, some are abroad but they keep in touch.

I'm not bitter or dried up and I don't think any jealous thoughts about other women being married. To me, life had more to offer than cleaning a house and fetching and carrying for a man. I have always been on my own but this has given me independence. I've always had to sort things out for myself.

☐ I often look back on my life. Well, at ninety-one years old there's not much else to do. As a child I helped my mam wash overalls for navvies, we called them tax dodgers, but then we went to Nottingham where I trained as a lacemaker. I then married a miner and came to live in Denaby as he worked at the pit there. We had a

Balby High Road before the tram lines were laid in 1902. The building on the left became the old library

house in Old Wellgate in Conisbrough, they've knocked all the old houses and cottages down now and built flats.

☐ I originally come from Hyde Park but when I married my husband, he was a railway driver and we set up home in Wheatley. He died when he was forty. I felt as if I'd lost my right arm – he is my most treasured memory.

☐ I've been widowed since I was thirty-seven and I'm eighty- five now. I've been on my own all that time. I didn't want another husband, I might have got one who drank a lot and I wouldn't want that.

☐ My father was killed in the first war and then me and my younger brother were put up for adoption when our mother died shortly afterwards. My only memory of her was her beautiful auburn hair. My brother was adopted first and his new parents changed his name to theirs and I lost contact with him, although some years ago he got in touch with me again. Strangely enough his daughter has exactly the same name that my own daughter has; Elizabeth Anne. We met once or twice but gradually lost touch again because we no longer had anything in common.

The people who adopted me were very good to me. My adoptive father had known my mother and at one time had wanted to marry her. They had another daughter who was fourteen years older than me. She was a bit schoolmarmish and I suppose you could say hard. My adoptive mother was lovely though, she said that I brought sunshine into her life.

They taught me to drive when I was seventeen, I was still at school at the time. That was in the early thirties. Father's first car was a Morris and there weren't many cars about then and even fewer women drivers. My mother was a much better driver than my father. He was a deputy at the pit but I think they also had inherited money because they always had smashing cars. Everybody stared as we drove past.

As he was going upstairs one night, carrying a big stone hot water bottle, he slipped and hit his head on the stairs. It caused a brain haemorrhage and he died.

☐ I do treasure memories of my childhood. There were just six boys and seven of us girls living in Barnburgh which is just a small village. We used to tap on the farrier's window and run away. He'd come out and shout, "Man or lad, you'll get some whip." Then he'd come running after us with his horse whip.

Barnburgh was also a place of legends. "The man killed the cat and the cat killed the man." Percy Cressacre came home on his horse and a wild cat jumped on his back. He made it back to the church porch and as he took his last breath he kicked out and killed the cat. As a child that tale used to both fascinate and frighten me.

☐ I was born in Mexborough in 1920 and went to Armthorpe School. My husband was a miner, he came from Armthorpe and though I was widowed at forty, we had three children. They come and visit me here in the Marshalls. In between visits I enjoy watching television and reading romantic novels.

☐ My mother-in-law was always a teetotal, church going woman. She wouldn't have any alcohol under any circumstances and as she got older she got more set in her ways. She got to seventy without ever having a drink.

We had some friends who had a pub near Leeds and hearing that a family of entertainers called The Wallace Family, who were supposed to be a good act, were appearing at the pub, we persuaded my mother-in-law to come with us. We got ourselves set up at this table in front of the stage; the place was so packed it was the only one left. Orders were taken for drinks, just as we were about to say, "Your usual orange, Mum?" – a chap walked past the table carrying two glasses of Pimms. The glasses were full of fruit and topped off with a bunch of violets.

Her eyes lit up. "That's what I want," she said. "Are you sure?" we asked. She wasn't just sure, she was positive. The first one went down and I don't think it touched the sides of her throat before she was tapping her fingers on the table ready for the next drink. "That was beautiful, I'll have the same again." After four of these the band was in full swing and so was mother.

I was watching the drummer and I thought the poor chap had some sort of affliction. His head kept jerking and he would slap his chest then his neck. What courage, I thought, to perform in public in his condition. It was only when I glanced across at my mother-in-law that I found out why he was afflicted. She had saved all the pips out of the orange and lemon pieces and was sitting flicking them towards the stage, they hit the target every time. The target was the drummer.

When we left she was very unsteady on her feet, but for weeks after she told everyone what a wonderful night out she'd had. We didn't have the heart to tell her it wasn't just fruit cup she'd been drinking.

They're Not Kids Any More

☐ My children are thirty-five years and forty-one years old now, but I still worry over their troubles although my husband keeps reminding me that they're not kids anymore. And he's right you know, so I don't interfere.

☐ "I never had a middle-age, I had a baby instead." I say this sometimes when I hear women moaning about being forty or fifty. I suppose I've been in the wrong age group many times because I married lateish and became a mother when lots of my contemporaries were just sampling the joys of being grandparents. I know it's normal and healthy to become parents when younger but sometimes there's no choice and there is something very special about a

I was 5 and my brother Frank was 6 on this school photo

Growing old started younger in those days

On my mother's knee

late child. Even more so when it's a one and only child.

The family was the keystone of my life and I never doubted that one day I'd have my own family. I'd already chosen the names for the first six boys, when an ectopic pregnancy nearly cost me my life and my chances of conceiving again were considerably reduced. I was forced to take stock of my life at that point and had frequent bouts of gloom and doom.

I was teaching in a girls' school when I married and after a long bout of ill health I returned to teaching. At forty I was working with handicapped children and old age seemed just round the corner. At forty-one – surprise, surprise! I was pregnant. I hardly dared tell anyone though in case it was a mistake or something awful happened so I just hoped and prayed and worried. In the meantime I collected family photographs and started a family album and traced the family tree back as far as I could, hoping to add my 'late bloom' to the bunch.

In my fifties, cycle rides, ballet and tap lessons, swimming, horse riding and Youth Hostelling were pleasures I shared with my daughter. In Youth Hostels it was a positive advantage to have done it all before. There's no substitute for experience and it's great to be able to produce a slap-up meal when everyone else is struggling with tin openers.

Now sixty-one, though I've no ambition to be the oldest swinger in town, I have graduated to disco dancing and recently entered the night club scene because my daughter now has a vacation job in one. She's doing a degree course in geography and will, I hope, have an Honours degree at the end of it.

☐   We had two boys who are both in business. They and their wives are very good to me. I don't think if I'd had any daughters it would have made any difference, I've had so much pleasure out of my boys.

Queen Street decorated for Balby Feast.

A street party in Balby to celebrate King George V and Queen Mary's Silver Jubilee

☐ My kids have given me some of the best moments. I've a lovely son, I never see him, though he rings me sometimes. I once surprised him. He was going to work in Venezuela and I wanted to see him. I saw advertised on television a special one pound rail ticket. So I set off early from Doncaster and changed at London made my way across by tube then on to Brighton where he was living at the time. I stayed three hours and then went back home the same day. I'd be about seventy-seven years old at the time.

☐ My children have been good to me, always nudging me. I was a creature of habit. The lad came in one Thursday and said, "What, Thursday and no meat and potato pie?" I must get out of this routine I thought.

They were very good after my husband died as well. I'd always been able to make do and mend. After he went I couldn't be bothered and let things go. The lad sympathised but my daughter geed me up and showed me how to live again.

One year, the lad told me to bring a big case for my Christmas present. I thought I would be getting a dressing gown but I was wrong, it was a return ticket to Canada to visit my cousins. The girl was very practical; if my stair carpet was worn, there would be a new one when I got home.

I wouldn't say I was strict with children, though I am a disciplinarian. I don't like this new idea of letting kids do as they please. I'm dogmatic, if I told the kids to do something, I'd expect them to do it. My daughter once went running out without taking her cod liver oil. I said, "It'll be two at dinnertime, love." Back she came. I wouldn't give an inch with my children, I never let them put one over me. I like children if they are well behaved. I don't like this modern way of bringing them up with no discipline.

☐ I'm no prude. My kids were growing up in the fifties and sixties and I used to love it with a house full of kids and their friends, listening to records and drinking coffee. But when they went down to London, sharing flats with umpteen others − then I used to worry.

☐ I've been widowed twice, two children by each husband. They're all grown up now and I've been on my own for twenty-odd years, since my daughter got married. I've got used to living on my own, no choice. Don't see much of the kids now, though three of them still live close.

One of my sons lives in Ellesmere Port, of course he doesn't get over to see me very often. It was two years since he'd last been, so I phoned and said I wanted him to come over. It takes a lot to make me mad but I'd been saving it up and really let him have it. A phone call once a month just to let me know he was all right and still alive was all I needed.

He just sat there on the settee and listened to me rant on and didn't say much, then after a bit he got up and went. He always was on the quiet side. Before he left he said he'd give me a ring but whether or not he will, I don't know and it'll probably be another two years before I see him again.

I used to go and visit them as often as I could, especially when my grandson was ill, before he died. I travelled over there a lot but the biggest problem now is changing trains in Liverpool. I've had arthritis for years, I've never let it get me down but the last three or four years it's got much worse. I spend two or three months in hospital in Buxton each year and have these gold injections for my joints, but I can't move fast enough to tackle the escalators or to trudge up and down all those stairs. It wears me out. The last time I went it took me five hours, I was so weary when I got to my son's house, all I could do was sit down. Then after tea it was time to set off home again and I still hadn't recovered from the journey getting there. I was three days in bed when I got home.

Now I think it's about time my kids came to see me instead of expecting me to do all the visiting so I said all this to my son. "Well you should have said something," he said.

But good heavens the last thing I want is to be constantly asking. I've taken care of myself most of my life but sometimes children just don't think. I don't expect any of them to be running round after me, they don't need to call everyday, I don't want that either, I just want them to phone occasionally and come and see me from time to time.

I've always been one for getting about. When my legs were all right, I couldn't keep in, tripping off into town on market days, off visiting, going down to the club, but I can't get around like I used to, I miss that. Done my share of visiting in the past, could do with a few visitors myself now.

My God, this must make me sound as if I'm really sorry for myself. A real old misery. Life's had its ups and downs but there's been lots of laughs on the way and I'm not ready to leave it yet. But kids, well, they never stop being a worry to you long after they're too big to clip round the ear.

☐ After my first marriage broke up I started courting Brenda. She had a car so she'd leave it outside my mother's when we were going out because, of course, we'd just go in one car. One evening we got back and it was teeming with rain. We parked outside the house and were just planning a kiss and cuddle when this 'benny hat' appeared and these knuckles rapped on the side window. I wound it down and a finger poked through at Brenda and said, "You want to watch that lad," then the finger poked at me and said, "And you watch yourself."

Mum must have been waiting ages for the car to appear because she was absolutely saturated. It wouldn't have been so bad if I hadn't been in my fifties at the time, and mum was seventy-odd. Brenda and I eventually got married but it took mum a long time to come round.

A Home Of Your Own

☐ I've never been as happy since I got my bungalow. The wardens are lovely and

Balby Road near St John's Church

68

Albany Road is typical of turn of the century housing in Doncaster

really do look after you. I think everybody should have the opportunity of a bungalow when they retire. It would be a better way of spending money instead of on tax cuts for rich folk. I know some put a lot of value on their independence but your own house with lots of furniture isn't everything. You can take your memories into a bungalow. I'd never go in a home, though.

☐ The house my grandmother lived in was a terraced pit house. The only floor covering was a dark pegged rug in front of the fire. The floor was quarry tiles, there was an old pot sink with a cold water tap and next to it was a copper. The only furniture in the living kitchen was a large scrubbed top table and three old wooden dining chairs. At either side of the fire stood wooden rocking chairs, they didn't have cushions just the hard wooden seats. Comfort was almost non-existent.

☐ I was the first tenant in the bungalows

around here and I believe that I'm also the longest tenant. The only thing I don't like about the bungalows is the open plan gardens. I would like a bit of ground to call my own and also my own backyard. I suppose this stems from living in a house for forty-four years.

☐ Old folk's homes are all right. They're not too depressing, it's just the folk that are in them. I'll carry on managing by myself while ever I can.

☐ I was seventy when I bought my first home; that was nineteen years ago. It's in Earlesmere Avenue and it cost me six-hundred pounds. I'm not too fond of cooking, though. I just do cheese on toast and simple things. I was used to being cooked for so I never learned how to bake a cake or anything and I still don't know how to.

When I went to The Marshalls old people's home for lunch, I looked round

He lost his fight to stay in his family home

High rise flats can be a lonely place to live

and thought, "The poor miserable old things," and most were younger than me.

☐ I live in a bungalow now. My wife died and so did one of my sons, the other son is married so I was on my own. Trouble with bungalows they are built in rows; my front looks on to the next row's backs. At night you can't see any lights on, I used to think they'd all gone out but they've not, they're all watching TV in the front room.

The bungalows are very cold in winter and I can't afford radiators on all day but I put one on in the bedroom about an hour before bedtime or else the room would be too cold to go into. They ought to allow us a bit more fuel. What's a fiver? You can burn that in a day, and it's got to be one degree below freezing point before we can claim that.

In summer the bungalows are too hot. You can open all the doors but you are still sweltered to death. Too many glass windows, that's the trouble, and they are too big. There's nothing worse than glass for drawing the sun. Mind you, I can grow all my own tomatoes on the windowsill. Big and sweet they are.

☐ My sister and I put our names down for flats at the same time; we moved here about the same time and live opposite each other. It's lovely to have each other's company but it's also nice to be able to close our own front doors if we want to. The flats are lovely, the warden looks in once a day and we have home helps to do the floors and windows, although we do the rest of the housework ourselves.

It's a pity no pets are allowed in the flats. If you've got one when you come here you can keep it but if it dies, you're not allowed to replace it. I love cats but I realise it's not practical to keep one in a flat, and being in a top flat, there's a lot of doors and I wouldn't want to keep having to go up and down stairs continually to let it in or out.

There's not generally too much trouble

with vandals and hooligans around here. There used to be but there's less now. We're up at the posh end where it's more private.

The rent for these flats is twenty-four pounds a week including rates, so that's not too bad. I got a bill for home insurance this morning, though, for twenty-eight pounds, it's quite a bit of money to find out of my pension and I had been thinking of cancelling it, but then a few weeks ago three bungalows near the Community Centre caught fire and were gutted, so I thought better of it and paid the insurance.

You don't think your belongings are worth a great deal till you stop to think of the cost of replacing them should something like that happen. It puts twenty-eight pounds a year into perspective then. I just don't think it's worth the risk because a fire doesn't have to be your own fault. It was the middle bungalow where the fire started but it spread to the ones on either side. You can take all the care in the world, but you can't stop something like that happening.

☐ I'd go into a home if I had to but only if I couldn't do for myself, otherwise I'll stick it out here in this council house. No, I don't fancy moving in with relations, don't want to be beholden to anyone really, especially my own.

☐ I hope I don't have to end my days in a home or hospital. Although they seem well looked after I don't think I could take it. On the other hand, if I ended up staying with any of my children I would like them to make me a bedsitting room, then I wouldn't get on their nerves and I could cop out if they got on mine. But if ever I become a burden on my family I suppose I'll have to go in a home. I got used to community living during the war, I could get used to it again.

☐ I'm living with my daughter but she is having trouble with her heart. I suffer with Parkinson's disease and if the time comes when I can't look after myself I want to go into The Marshalls. I know I'll be all right there.

The Old Folks' Home

☐ I never thought I'd like it in a home but after a few days I settled myself down. Everybody gets treated alike, there's no fish and feathers in here. I didn't want to give up my house, I lived in Barnburgh all my life, but the hospital advised me to come here for six weeks and I've never been back. The staff are very patient and try to help us keep our independence, encouraging us to do things for ourselves.

☐ I come to the Marshalls two days a week to sort of get used to the idea of residential homes because I expect to have to go in one when I get a bit older. But then I hope to go in the Ridings at Edlington. I love Fridays here, especially dinner. It's fish and chips followed by apple crumble. The Marshalls have the best cook around here. Mind you, she's not the cook my mother was. She was cook up at St Catherine's Hospital until she was sixty. She retired and then they asked her to go back. She worked there up to being eighty years old. She taught me to cook, my Yorkshire puddings are lovely and I often cook one of them turkey roasts and two veg. Aye, I can make a good dinner, no tinned muck for me.

☐ I have only come to The Marshalls for two weeks. I am on my second week and I've enjoyed every minute of it. I was a bit troubled, you see, when I knew I was coming. I thought it was a hospital but it's lovely. I'm treated proper, no one shouts and bawls at us, the staff are very nice and look after us very well.

☐ I lived in a bungalow before I came to live in an old people's home. It became too difficult for me to shop and get about and look after myself but I've never regretted coming here. It's nice to have company if you want it, and if you want to be private you can go into your own bedroom so I have the best of both worlds.

☐ I'm not really keen on old folks'

The Marshalls

homes. There was a lovely old lady who used to come to our community centre, now she's gone into the home we never see her. She's just thrown in the towel — it's heart-breaking.

☐ I've lived at the Marshalls for about a year and I've settled down well and made some good friends. After living on my own for a number of years I enjoy the company, it's much better than being alone. I don't think I would change my life, really. I am quite content where I am. I enjoy the company here and have many friends.

☐ I cried when I had to come to The Marshalls but soon learned to live here. My three daughters used to have me with them in their homes. But they're all in their sixties and seventies now and of course, they are all troubled with illnesses, so I came here. If I feel a bit depressed I go and sit in the foyer because I can't brood and let things bother me. I don't get my pension but I have eight pounds a week pocket money. If I need anything my daughters fetch it for me, they are good lasses, they come to see me every week.

I have my own place at the table at meal times. They don't announce it if anyone in here dies, but if we ask, the staff will sometimes tell us. On a Sunday the vicar comes and we have a service.

☐ If anybody gets out, folk round here know where they're from, but you can't blame them for wanting to get out, just for a walk sometimes. We're not too badly done to, though. At Christmas Woolworth gave a 40lb box of chocolates to be distributed among us inmates.

☐ If anybody had told me that I'd live till I was ninety-two I wouldn't have believed them. I get despondent with ill health and not being able to get out. I can't walk and sometimes it's too hot and stuffy in here. Some want the windows open and some want them shut. I must have dropped off this morning and spilt my tea. I never know what day it is except on a Sunday when they have a service.

☐ I lived in Stirling Street until I was in my sixties. Then I was fortunate to get one of Nuttall's Cottage Homes in Bennethorpe. I'm now in my nineties and I've finished up at The Marshalls residential home. I've got used to it, I've had to because I don't expect to be moving anywhere else.

☐ I used to be the stewardess at Ashmount Club, I was there for twenty-four years and at the same time my husband was a bookie, he ran a betting shop in Balby. We lived in a flat above the club and I did the cleaning and bar work and had a cellarman to do the heavy work. I retired when I was forty-eight and was widowed nine years ago.

My eyesight gradually started to go not long after I retired and now I can't read or write or watch television. I have arthritis in my leg and now I can't walk very far but I've never mixed much. When I came to The Marshalls three years ago I wanted to make a clean break so I brought my favourite chair with me and nothing else apart from photos of my eight brothers and sisters. I have a niece who comes to visit me, but that's the trouble with living too long – everybody's gone before.

☐ I've never been interested in marriage, I'm all right on my own. I lived on my own for years after the death of both parents. I had my own home in Bentley Road. It had three bedrooms and a lot of steps, so when it became too much for me I came to live in The Marshalls. I made a clean break when I came. I'd no regrets about giving up my home. I left all my furniture and things and all I brought with me is some photographs of relatives and friends. The food is good in here and I never liked cooking much anyway. That was about three years ago and I like it here now I've got to know them. They are very friendly but I was never one for mixing much. I'd like it better in a home just for women though.

☐ I don't want to end up in a home if I can help it. I don't like the way they mix the lively with the senile. I reckon they should have separate homes for people who have physical disabilities but still have their wits about them and if they decline into senility they should then be moved into a home specially for the senile. It's not fair to mix them like they do. The senile ones might not know the difference but the others do and I would find it very depressing being lumped together with people who can't laugh, talk sense or understand where they are, just because my arthritis has gotten so bad I can't carry on living in my own home.

☐ I had trouble with my nerves so I moved out of my flat at Wheatley Hill and for a short while went into a private home. But then I was ill and had to go into hospital and when I came out I came to The Marshalls. I didn't like it at first, it was strange but I've got used to it now.

I knew Vera from many years ago so it was nice to see a familiar face when I came and we sometimes go into Doncaster or Sheffield together. I used to go every week but Vera doesn't enjoy it as much so I don't go so often now. However I do occasionally go out for a drink with Karen, one of the officers in charge, and some of the nurses, after they've finished work here on Saturday nights. We have bingo every Thursday night here and I win often enough to keep myself in bubble bath and talc, and the hairdresser comes twice a week so I always make a point of having my hair done.

When I came here last year I brought my bed, wardrobe and a set of drawers, my electric sewing machine, a small television and a few pictures that I've had a long time.

My husband and I separated a few years ago so I'm in The Marshalls and he's in Stenson Court residential home. It's as well he isn't in the same place that I am. There is one married couple living here and they row like the devil and everybody hears – there's not enough privacy here for domestic disagreements.

In summer I like to go walking to

Hexthorpe Flatts and I play bowls with some of the old chaps. My mother taught me to play, she was a good bowls player and once won a cup when we were still living in Nottingham.

It's a pity there aren't more activities here but it is difficult getting some of them interested, I've found that out for myself. Another problem is that they stopped my supplementary pension when I came here and they take my old age pension and give me 8.25 spending money every week, which unfortunately doesn't go far when you smoke. I've had to cut back and I'm down to about four cigarettes a day.

It's nice to see kids coming in here with visitors. I like to see them playing and they bring some life into the place. It's a pity there are no dogs, though; it's well recognised that pets are good for old people. There's a couple of budgies, I help to look after them, but it's not the same. I could have had a dog if all the residents had agreed to it but they didn't.

I'm not really complaining. These days we should count ourselves lucky. Until a few years ago when the local authority started providing residential homes, the only alternative for old folk who couldn't look after themselves and if their children didn't take them in, was the workhouse.

☐   I was brought up in the workhouse — or Western Hospital as they called it. Then I went to live at Haynes House in Thorne. It was nice I used to help with washing up and a bit of cleaning. I can give it a good character, the people who run it are very nice you know, no bullying or hitting, very kind.

I've been in Shadyside now for the past six years and I'm quite happy. I have my own television and chest of drawers and I'm right proud of them. They are the first things I've ever owned. I can go out when I want to and have a choice of meals even though I'm a diabetic. I wish I had a bible though. My Dad and Mam always had one but I've never owned one — never owned much at all.

Hexthorpe Flatts

Still Rambling.

Stephen McClarence

Enough Insurance

Old Fashioned Remedies

☐ I do think about death. When I get up in a morning and feel ninety, I have a cup of tea and hope that it will wear off.

☐ I still have a healthy appetite and bake my own fruitcakes, I don't deprive myself. I enjoy a cigarette and always have a spot of whisky in my first cup of tea on a morning; it gets the blood circulating.

You've got to keep moving about when you get older; let your limbs go stiff and you might as well be dead. Some folk are well looked after as they get older, to hear others talk you'd think they get nothing and everybody else everything, but you can't rely too much on other folk helping.

☐ It's hard when your partner has gone. It's too easy to give up and just wait for death. I want to be buried with my husband, he was a grand lad, but in the meantime I like company, I like mixing with people. It's an effort sometimes but it's important. It helps to keep the old brain working.

☐ I don't think you're ever too old to have a bit of fun and enjoy yourself. Naturally our bodies do wear out and sometimes memories get a bit bad but I still think we are responsible for a lot of our actions. I can say this, though, because I'm only in my early sixties but at present there's nothing better for me than a good laugh, better than anything we can get from the doctors.

☐ When I feel a bit down I sing to myself. You know, what they call the oldies. Can't do with today's music if that's what they call it – it sounds like a lot of screaming tom cats to me. No, give me the old ballads every time, good words and good tunes. Well they must be good, they are still sung today and some of them were written when I was only a sparkle in my dad's eye.

☐ Whenever I reach an all-time low, I give myself a choice between work or worry! I choose work every time and that's why I've always been an active busy person.

Ailments And Old Age

☐ I had polio when I was two. That would be in 1906 and the treatment then was to cut the tendons in my foot and ankle. I wore a calliper for about twenty years till my leg was strong enough, and though I've had no need for one for the last sixty-odd years, I still walk with a dropped foot because of that operation. I can't imagine what good it was supposed to do, but then there were other treatments in those days that seem barmy now. For instance, before the war my sister-in-law had a nervous breakdown of sorts. The doctor's answer to that was to tell her to have all her teeth out. A fat lot of good that did.

I was late starting school with having polio and the sort of calliper I wore didn't have a hinge at the knee so they had a special chair made for me at school to support my leg.

☐ I can't think why people insist that years ago were the good old days, I don't think they were. For instance, my dad died of pneumonia. There was no cure then, not like today with a lot more medicines and treatment.

☐ One can't be too independent, it's being independent that keeps you going. I can't do with folk that are insincere, I say what I think or say nothing. I don't take any tablets of any sort, they have too many side effects – don't trust them.

My next door neighbour has had this gammy leg since he was fourteen. He got it playing football, he broke his right knee and it was never set properly. He is now over sixty and it's getting worse so the doctor told him it was time something was done about it. So three years ago he had an artificial knee joint put in.

The new joint broke after a couple of weeks. The replacement joint wasn't in long before it worked loose and started locking, so it was taken out and a pin put in to straighten up his leg. Unfortunately he had lots of infection in it and ended up with a pot from thigh to ankle with holes drilled in it through to the bone — but then the screws worked loose and he got more infection in it. He reckons he's had more penicillin than Fleming.

Next they tried a locator, which is two pins into the lower thigh bone and two pins into the shin bone with a metal rod to keep it rigid. The knee joint is now missing so the two ends should now join up. So he's going to end up with a still leg which will be a good bit shorter than his other leg.

He's currently on crutches but he wasn't cheered up much when a doctor walked past and commented — "About time that leg was taken off." And he reckons they probably will take it off before they've finished. After three years of surgery and pain — and they still haven't finished with him, he says he was better off with his gammy leg.

My worst problem is my hiatus hernia, I keep getting acid coming up, so I have my bed on bricks. The doctor told me I have to keep my head above my stomach to keep the acid down. They gave me a barium meal, if I had to have that again I think I'd sooner go now. Drinking cups of pink stuff while the doctor took photos of my gullet and told me not to belch.

Cancer is one of my worries, my husband, daughter and mother all died of it. I'm quite prepared to go, but I wouldn't want to suffer like my husband did. If somebody told me I was going tomorrow I'd be ready for it. God's given me strength and a lucky life but we've all got to go sometime.

They made a special chair for me at school.

78

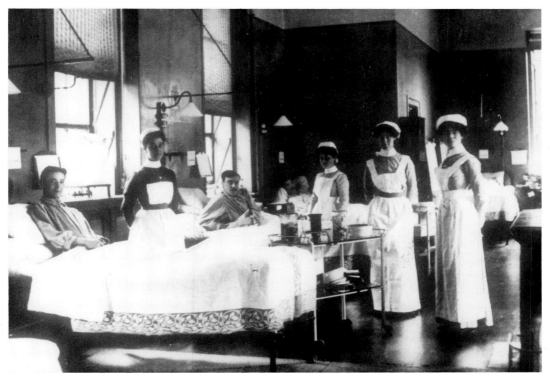

The Royal Infirmary closed in 1933 and became Education Offices

☐ I'm not well. Everybody thinks I am because I'm lively, but it's a great effort to get out of bed and make breakfast every morning. While I can get upstairs to my room and toilet I will, I go up like a monkey. Sometimes I wake up and say, "Ooh I'm dead" – and I'm a bit disappointed when I find I'm not.

I wouldn't mind dying one bit but I don't want to suffer. I'd like to sit down and go to sleep. When you get to eighty- nine you're on the last lap. I feel as though I don't want to live much longer to be completely honest. Sometimes when I sit down and doze off, I come round and wonder what day it is, what time it is and what I've been doing; that's a bit frightening.

☐ When the National Health came in, it was 1948, Bevan said they would look after people from cradle to grave. What a mistake. It was greatly misused. They'd spend far more on bus fares to get a one inch bandage than it would have cost them to buy

one, but they did it because they thought they were getting something for nothing. It was the same with surgical gauze and lint. They'd get it by the yard on the National Health and then make curtains and things with it.

Everyone was scrambling for glasses and teeth and they got them whether they needed them or not. What Bevan ought to have done was give a little bit at first, and then kept on adding a bit more. But they got too much at once. I know there's two sides to every story but there always will be some reckless people, and being a pharmacist I was very aware of the waste.

☐ I had a hysterectomy when I was seventy. That was twenty-one years ago, and afterwards they gave me a flat in Brookside in Conisbrough. It's a lovely spot and I was very happy there. The people were very friendly, there was never any bickering.

My husband died at the age of seventy-seven. After he'd had an operation I had to nurse him for years, it was hard work for me because by then I was seventy-five.

When I was ninety I had to have an operation on my eyes for cataracts. At first they said there was nothing wrong with my eyes it was all in my mind, but they ended up operating. I'm glad they did because at ninety-one years old I can still get about under my own steam, and to me that's very important.

☐　I'm seventy-three now, and I had a stroke four years ago and I still haven't got over it properly. I can't do the housework like I used to do or get about so much now — and I used to be a keen walker.

☐　I live on my own in a bungalow but I've come to the Marshalls for a fortnight's respite. I think that's what they call it. You see I had a fall in Doncaster. It didn't half shake me up. My arm's in a right mess, all black and blue. Someone said it was broke but I don't think it is, no swelling you see.

I fell over a paving stone that was stuck up, I think Doncaster pavements are disgusting. Of course, if we say anything or complain they say it's the cut-backs. A few years ago a friend of mine had a bad fall same as me. She tried to claim compensation and had to supply photographs and drawings and all sorts of trouble she had to put up with. It took her four years to get her claim sorted out and she'd the union to back her up at that.

I went to Benidorm once and their pavements are lovely, they're flat and even and done in lovely colours. They were doing a lot of building though, well, I'm saying building they seemed to be throwing them up.

I've got to go to the infirmary today, in fact I'm waiting for the ambulance but don't know how long I'll be waiting — it could be half a day. I hope I'm not waiting too long at the hospital, sometimes it takes all day. It's a good job they are sending someone with me, at least I'll have somebody to talk to.

☐　If there comes a time when my legs won't make it up and down the stairs, I'll do

Relaxing on the beach

Infirmary Sunday parade

as my mother-in-law used to do, I'll go up and down on my bottom.

☐   I always say that I'm a little walking gold mine because I've had so many gold injections for rheumatoid and osteo-arthritis. My hands are crippled and walking isn't easy either, and now it's affecting my sight. Life isn't made any easier with all these childproof caps on bottles.

I know children have to be protected but you'd think that with things like tablets they'd give you a choice when you pick up your prescription. If you've no children about the house then you should be able to get ordinary bottle caps. I have so much trouble getting the caps off, I either end up with the tablets all over the floor, or being unable to take any because I can't get them off at all. It's the same with biscuit packets. By the time I get them open, I'm left with a pile of broken ones.

☐   Retirement meant the end of work related stress. But having retired before I was sixty-five and needing a regular prescription from my doctor, I found that although I was living on a pension, I was not allowed free medicines.

☐   When my grandmother was well into her eighties, she was still going out everyday, collecting the pensions and doing odd jobs for the other old people in the village. She was fit and healthy right up to the end and then she went to bed one night and died during the night − no warning, no indication. That's the way to go − that's the way I want to go too.

☐   My Auntie Susie was quite fit until recently. Then in March she went into hospital with cancer of the bowel. It had come on relatively suddenly, she hadn't been feeling ill for very long. They took away part of her bowel and discharged her after only four weeks. She was discharged far too soon but they said they needed her bed for other acute cases. Perhaps someone else had been discharged too soon to make way for Auntie Susie because she didn't have to wait for her operation. I suppose that's one way for the National Health to keep the waiting lists short, but she wasn't fit to be discharged.

The hospital did arrange for the Home Help service to resume her three hours per week but that was a poor substitute for the full time nursing care that she needs. She needs to go to the loo four or five times in a couple of hours and now, since the operation she's not so good on her legs and walks with a zimmer frame, she can't always get there in time and sometimes she's been found in a sorry state. Though I give great credit to her Home Help. When she saw how the situation was with Auntie Susie she took it on her own back to go in every morning and that has now been made official. But Home Helps don't work weekends.

If old people are going to be ill they really should avoid being ill at weekends, or failing that they should give them an injection on Fridays that knocks them out till Mondays when the Home Help Service resumes again. It's a diabolical state of affairs for Auntie Susie and all other old people in a similar situation. It says nothing for our so called Welfare State.

☐ My husband had ill health due to an accident in the pit. I had to look after him and go out to work as well because I never knew when he would feel well enough to work. Now I'm retired society tries to throw me on the scrap heap but I'm not having it.

☐ I don't like getting old. I've always led such an active life and hate not being able to do all the things I want to any more. I find myself putting things off till tomorrow because I can't face doing them. I know it's important to keep the body and senses going as much as you can, the trouble is that while my mind is okay my body is giving out. People live too long these days.

Funeral at the Primitive Methodist Chapel on Carr House Road

A nap before tea

Euphamisms And Euthanasia

☐ I'm not ready to go just yet but I'm not frightened of dying. In any case, if I thought I was going to go funny in my old age I'd rather cock my clogs. Best way to go is in your sleep but I believe in euthanasia when there's no hope of recovery. It's pointless letting people suffer. When they're down to skin and bone or don't know what day it is they should give them something to help them on their way.

☐ Most old people will have given euthanasia some thought. I've never been able to say yes or no, but I suppose if people were given a special tablet to take in an emergency, after a certain age, a lot would take it.

☐ I don't agree with putting old folk to sleep, with all the medicines and what have you that they've got these days there's no need for it. Where there's life there's hope. Anyway homes are provided for old folk who can't look after themselves.

☐ I'm a firm believer in euthanasia, at eighty-nine I know I'll not get any better, I can only get worse, so I'll not be sorry when it's time for me to go.

I wanted to go into a residential centre for the elderly but they say I'm too fit, I can still look after myself. I'm always being told how well I look but nobody sees the difficulties behind the smiles.

☐ I'm not frightened of dying. Death comes and we can't stop it, but when it does, I hope I go quick. I don't want to become a cabbage. The thing that bothers me most about dying is when I see how people treat furniture and belongings that have been left. I haven't got a lot of treasures but the few I have mean a lot to me and to think that somebody might break them up or push them in a dustbin after I've gone is a bit upsetting. I've seen it done with some of my friends.

When I was younger I never thought of death but now I realise it's coming up fast, especially now I know I've had my three score and ten.

I believe in enjoying life while you can and die whenever you're ready. I've no belief in God or an afterlife. If there is any sort of afterlife, though, I hope I don't go to heaven. I've a friend who is a strong believer in God and believes that when we go to heaven we spend our afterlife praising God. How boring. I firmly believe that it's curtains – nothing follows. I don't want anything else.

I'm not given over to thinking much about death, as long as there's enough money to give me a decent burial. There won't be much for frills or anything fancy. I don't want them bringing me flowers, it's a waste if you ask me. Well, I won't be there to see them will I? No, if they want to bring me flowers I'd just as soon have them now so I can have the pleasure of them. And I don't want a stone on my grave, they won't need to hold me down because I've no intention of coming back again.

Going Out In Style

As a child I remember this really impressive funeral. The coach which carried the coffin was pulled by four black horses with black plumes. It must have been the funeral of one of the rich folk from the big house because only rich people had so many horses and such a fancy funeral. I was so impressed by the sight of it that more than anything, I wanted a black horse for myself. The village children ran behind the funeral shouting and cheering, thinking it was a parade.

I sometimes worry if I've enough insurance to cover my funeral but my son always says, "Get your money spent Mam, we can always bury you in the back yard." I've got to laugh at him.

My mother is in her eighties and she has always been smart in her appearance.

Doncaster Workhouse at Balby later became Western Hospital but the stigma remained. It is now demolished and a housing estate stands on the site.

84

Parkinson's produced other things than butterscotch during the war

She won't go to the community centre without putting make-up on. One day she was sitting talking to me and the conversation took on a sombre note, she started talking about when she died. Completely seriously she said, "I want you to promise me you won't let them put me away without my make-up. I don't want to go up there looking a mess."

☐ I think it's ridiculous the price of funerals. I'm sure there must be huge amounts of profit made. I speak to our local undertaker whenever I see him but I don't like it if he asks me how I am. I can't help but think he's already measuring me up.

☐ I had a strict Catholic upbringing. At school we had sheets of blotting paper, the big blots were mortal sins, the small blots lesser sins.

I'm an agnostic now, I don't really know what I believe. One day a friend rang me up and said, "Do you ever think of dying?" I said I did and she answered, "Well I hope I don't go just now because I've got my teeth out and my curlers in, I look a real bonny bugger."

☐ We are insured against death but I don't know if it will be enough, I hope so. It's too expensive to die these days, but it comes to us all, doesn't it? Something we can't avoid. Mind you my grandad was buried in what they called a pauper's grave because the family didn't have enough money to bury him properly. I don't think they have them now.

☐ I was born in Doncaster but moved to Stafford when my husband got a job as superintendent of a crematorium. He's always worked in cemeteries or crematoriums and I've been in plenty of them myself. I know it's upsetting if it's one of your own you're visiting them for, but otherwise it's just a job. My husband always used to say, "I keep my eyes open and my mouth shut" − about what goes on in those places.

He died and was cremated at Stafford and his ashes were scattered around a tree at the crematorium, which had his name carved round the trunk. I'm not bothered whether I'm buried or cremated − they can please themselves once I'm gone.

☐ When I retired last year, I took part of my pension in a lump sum. At the time, the Co-op funeral department was running a promotion to encourage people to invest in their own funeral while they were still alive. The deal was that for every fifty pounds you invested towards your funeral, they would give you twenty-five pounds worth of vouchers to spend in their stores.

I invested five hundred pounds and the two hundred and fifty pounds of vouchers, I spent on a holiday in Yugoslavia at a naturist beach. After I'd booked the holiday, I still had enough vouchers left over to buy a French travelling bag − and got enough Co-op stamps with it to fill a book. I reckon I got a good deal for my money.

Any Regrets?

☐ Yes, I've had my regrets. If I had my time over again I wouldn't marry my late husband. I had to manage all our affairs. He had no go in him and no ambitions; no interests, too quiet and shy but I have always wanted to improve myself.

☐ I wish I'd married. I feel as if I've missed out not having a family. I rather fancy a son and daughter and perhaps now I would have a wife for companionship.

☐ I've never married. I've never had time nor inclination although I've had plenty of offers. No, I don't mind not having children. You can't always win if you do have kids. There's a woman in this old people's centre, she's been in here four years and neither son nor daughter have been to see her in that time.

☐ I joined up in the ATS during the war but if I had my time over again I wouldn't join up. I would be a conscientious objector. You realise as you get older that

Edlington colliery

86

He became a nationally celebrated photographer in his eighties

Stephen McClarence

we didn't fight for anything, really, just our own back yards.

I wouldn't get married either if I had another chance. Marriage should be a partnership and ours wasn't. He wasn't a wicked man but there was a lot of injustice. I never knew how much he earned, he just gave me housekeeping and never bought so much as a handkerchief for himself. Being in the forces taught me independence; he robbed me of it.

☐ If I had my time over again I'd go back in the peacetime army instead of spending forty years in Edlington pit.

☐ I never made any great plans for my life. I was born in 1927 and those days us girls were brainwashed into getting married and having a family. I have always regretted not being able to go to grammar school, and being stupid enough not to take up any further education. I did try further education about twenty years ago, but all I had offered me was a choice of knitting, sewing, cookery and flower arranging,

which I must say had no interest for me. In fact if I get out a needle and cotton my husband asks, "Who's got a splinter in their finger?"

I put my name down for a language class once. But there was only me interested so they cancelled the class. I guess I wasn't important enough.

☐ I think I'd have married another man if I had my time over again. Not that I didn't like the one that I had, I courted him eight years and idolised him. But I wanted to be somebody and he was a quiet shy man with no get up and go. I think I married him because he was good looking and wore tailor-made suits, he stood out from the other rough boys in Denaby. For all his looks, though, he had no idea. I had to do everything; I sorted out the bills and ran the shop that we had. If ever I left him in charge he'd give the wrong change, be rude to customers, he'd absolutely no idea.

I could have had somebody else. There was a young man went to Leeds University. He became a probation officer. If he'd been a bit more pushy he'd have knocked Walter out of the running.

☐ I'm still like an old mother hen. I want to cuddle my kids, but they've all fled the nest now so I cuddle my cat instead. My kids might think that they're too old for a cuddle but they're not − there's not enough love in the world today.

☐ I've never married, why should I look after a man? I know women who were very unhappy yet thought they were superior to me; because I was single they put me down. I have to laugh. I don't regret not having a companion, I had lots of boyfriends in my younger days but never followed anything up. If a new one came along I would go out with him. I've travelled all over Europe and had a good life without a man.

I'm not much of a housewife, I'm no cook and I'm not too fond of children or housework. I would much rather work for my living than be a wife and mother, though it's surprising how much people look down on spinsters − other women certainly do. But the warden who comes round says that spinsters are much more cheerful and pleasant to visit than any of the married women or widows so it must say something.

☐ I feel that the war took away a lot of opportunities for our age group. By the time the war was over it was too late for us to consider further education. There was no funding for courses unless you came from a wealthy family. We had to get jobs if we wanted to settle down with a family because once a woman got married, she automatically lost her job. Very few employers would take on a married woman.

☐ I used to have secret plans and dreams but they never came to anything. I would have liked to have been a singer. I'd a nice enough voice when I was young but I only got as far as entertaining the family and friends at parties. Never had the money to have my voice trained. I do like to listen to a good choir though and I love to hear a contralto singing.

☐ It's all gimme, gimme, gimme. I want this and I want that. The most I ever wanted was long curly hair.

A time to reflect